"Dear MAT

I hope You Found

Inspiration and memories

of a great night

Dude
You're
thankyou
being here and your help
and support as a bestman.

Cheers, Nathan

FOUR
KITCHENS

FOUR
KITCHENS

COLIN FASSNIDGE

EBURY
PRESS

To Jane, Lily and Maeve,
this book is for you.

CONTENTS

INTRODUCTION

I have been asked to write a book dozens of times over the past eight or so years, but I wasn't ready. I felt I needed to learn a lot more about cooking before I could share my ideas. Since then, I've had two children, Lily and Maeve, and it's because of them that I fell in love with cooking all over again ... and finally felt ready to write this book.

MY JOURNEY TO HERE

Family is almost always responsible for your initial feelings about food, and Irish family life revolves around the table. Growing up in Dublin, eating was a serious business, and my parents had designated days for cooking duties. My dad was Wednesdays and Sunday lunch, and my mum pretty much cooked the rest of the time.

My connection to food was fostered through my mother. Her day revolved around feeding the family. My brother Andrew and sister Elaine and I would get up, and Mum would make us breakfast. The weather was usually cold and miserable, so food needed to be hearty. Delia Smith was the celebrity chef when we were kids, and Mum tried to get trendy and cook things like courgettes. She succeeded, but what we really loved was the food that came naturally to her: offal. It was a treat. We always looked forward to it because she cooked those dishes so well – tasty and full of flavour. Dishes like liver and onion still take me right back to my childhood and I am still very heavily influenced by the food I ate as a youngster.

My dad was also a good cook. Super-organised. Our favourite Dad dishes were marrowfat peas (mushy peas), golden roasted potatoes, and roast beef (always well done – I'm not sure why, but he liked it that way). Prawn cocktails were huge in the 80s ... but he also made a mean trifle. Men in those days were hard: they didn't make trifles. Nevertheless, it was Dad's speciality and he was really proud of it. I think it's because of his appreciation of cooking that he encouraged me to become a chef. In those days, cooking as a career choice wasn't looked upon very well – it was seen as a bit of a drop-out job. Yet from the age of about twelve I wanted to be a chef. Or a zookeeper. Or a rock star. You could say that cooking professionally involves a combination of all of those things, so I reckon even back then I was on the money.

As much as I wanted to be a chef, I was a keen drummer. I worked part-time at my dad's shoe shop in the summer so that I could earn enough money to buy a drum kit. When I was fourteen, I had finally saved up enough to buy one. I was on fire – I joined a band and we even got on TV! The only problem was that in Dublin at that time everyone was in a band. So while it was a great time for music, the opportunities were slim. I grew my hair because I thought if you were in a band it was a pretty cool thing to do. Around the same time, I saw a documentary about chef Marco Pierre White. Long-haired, cigarette in one hand, knife in the other, he was losing it at the chefs in his kitchen and I thought, 'Cooking's cool.' Marco Pierre White was the first rock star chef. Nobody was doing anything like him.

I finished school and started at catering college the next year. I got to cook, and at that time the government gave you a grant if you were at catering college. Cook … and get paid? Yes! I figured that if I was doing something where I woke up every morning still keen, then it was the right thing for me.

THE DISCIPLINE OF BECOMING A CHEF

When I was at catering college, I met Kevin Thornton, who was one of my lecturers and pretty 'out there'. Kevin was leaving teaching to open a small restaurant called Thornton's and asked me to be a part of it. I said yes without even thinking and that's when my life went from pretty cushy to getting my arse kicked. There were four chefs, including Kevin, and within six months of opening Thornton's, Kevin received a Michelin star. I was below the pot wash in the scheme of things, so I got worked over from morning to night by the whole brigade. I had to make staff dinner every day, and this was the first place I learnt about discipline. In Ireland, we'd shoot our own deer. As a result, we had a lot of venison left over and we'd have it for staff meals. Venison is very lean, and therefore easy to overcook. I'd always overcook it and I'd always get caned for it.

Kevin promised me that if I stayed two years at Thornton's he'd get me a job in England. He knew I wanted to go there more than anything – it was my Emerald City. As a chef, it was where the gods of cooking worked: Marco Pierre White, Pierre Koffmann, Raymond Blanc. I stuck to my word and he stuck to his. He got me a job with Raymond Blanc and I flew over to Oxford. I started the same day as nine other apprentices. After a month, I was the only one left. I worked in a kitchen where nobody spoke to you for three months – there was no point getting to know you unless they knew you were good enough to be allowed to stay. I worked, slept for a handful of hours each night, and went back to work. I didn't take meal breaks or eat very much. I used to eat the chicken wings out of the stockpot like an animal. We didn't have time to do anything other than cook – the pressure was incredible. I worked like that for two years: sixteen-hour days, ten days on, one day off.

Those days weren't really about cooking, though. They were about following a routine and trying to stay out of trouble. I think what happens to a lot of people who want to become chefs is that they fall in love with the idea of creativity and using great produce, but then they get into a restaurant and realise that what they need to fall in love with is routine. You follow it and, though slow, the learning comes.

After three months with Raymond Blanc, I was accepted into the brigade, as I'd managed to outlast all the other junior chefs. Then it became like a band of brothers – there are guys from those days who I still keep in touch with. They're spread all over the world and many of them are incredibly successful. Justin North and I started together in the veg section and he is the reason I came to Sydney. He was a much better cook than me, too. (These days I'd like to think I give him a run for his money!)

Raymond Blanc was a self-taught chef who never went to college and ran a brigade of forty chefs. One of the greatest things he taught us (and it sounds obvious but not enough chefs do it) is to taste the food. Taste it, make an adjustment, taste it again. If there's one thing I ask you to take away from this book, it's to taste everything at every step of the way, and learn to find your own balance.

When I arrived in Sydney in 1999, Justin introduced me to Liam Tomlin, owner of Banc, and I started working there immediately. Unfortunately, Banc's not around anymore, and it's the kind of restaurant we'll never see again in Australia: twenty exceptional chefs in one kitchen. Banc was a beacon for those talented British chefs who wanted to move to Australia. Even now, Banc is regarded as one of the most remarkable restaurants that ever was. I don't think any other restaurant in the country bred as many high-calibre chefs. That restaurant and those people ... it was a moment in time. We worked really hard – and we enjoyed ourselves even harder.

FOUR IN HAND AND 4FOURTEEN

I started at the Four in Hand after a chance meeting with Joe Saleh. The Four in Hand was very highly regarded in 2004 when I started as the executive chef (it still is!). Its reputation was for pushing boundaries and winning awards, and it had garnered huge respect from its peers. Over its time, the Four in Hand has won and regained two chef hats and has been ranked in the top 30 restaurants in Australia by *Gourmet Traveller* magazine. My stress levels were through the roof maintaining that reputation, but I am really proud of it. When I opened 4Fourteen 8 years later, my wife, Jane, and I had had our two babies and I had mellowed a bit. Having kids puts things into perspective and I started to really taste food properly again. My style changed: it was no longer about perfect little dots on a plate, but about feeding people, providing an enjoyable experience. That's why I got into cooking in the first place. So nowadays I cook what I want to eat, not what's expected of me.

If you're going to do well as a chef it's because, in a small way, you've managed to delve into your childhood and pour some of those memories into your cooking. Our individuality comes from the sum of our life experiences. Taste can transport you back decades. Our ability to draw on nostalgia and bring it to the plate – a smell from childhood, a texture, a taste – that's a skill I regard highly among other chefs.

MY COOKING PHILOSOPHY

Bringing enjoyment to people is the most important thing you can do with your cooking.

I'm known for my love of nose-to-tail eating, using secondary cuts of meat, coaxing as much flavour out of the produce as possible and wasting as little as I can. I like to cook with local produce, using nature to inspire me, working hand in hand with local farmers and producers. My cooking has changed over the years. As I have got older, my style of cooking has become lighter. It has also become simpler; more about the quality of the ingredients and how best to showcase them, which is something I think you can only learn over time and through experimentation. Essentially, I think a chef's job is like a clown's – make people happy, bring a smile to their face, and they will leave with good memories.

THIS BOOK

This book is a collection of favourite recipes from both the Four in Hand and 4Fourteen, plus recipes I like to cook at home for family and friends. The title of the book, *Four Kitchens*, relates to the two restaurant kitchens, the bar or outside kitchen and the home kitchen.

These recipes are a guide only – how you interpret them is up to you. To me, recipe books are a collection of rectified mistakes. For every winning dish, a chef or cook has made at least ten mistakes to get there. So try these recipes. Succeed or fail. But think about the recipe, try it again and make it your own. Most importantly, never give up. That's how every single dish in this book came into being.

Colin Fassnidge

LIGHT BITES

Light bites came about from developing the menu at 4Fourteen. The menu there is structured into small plates you can share before moving on to the main event.

These plates are a little smaller than an entrée, but they set the mood for what's to come. This is where we grab you and intrigue you, and leave you wanting more – like a first date. They should be small portions, because you want people to still have an appetite so that they enjoy everything else you've prepared, and they should be exciting enough to be memorable long after dessert has been cleared from the table.

Light bites don't have to be the start of a long meal – they're equally great as snacks with a few glasses of wine.

CRAB TOAST

SERVES 2

INGREDIENTS

300g picked Alaskan King or Blue Swimmer crab meat
50g mayonnaise
1 spring onion, chopped
½ avocado, diced
¼ bunch flat-leaf parsley, leaves roughly chopped
¼ bunch chives, roughly chopped
pinch of smoked paprika
pinch of cayenne pepper
finely grated lemon zest and lemon juice, to taste
4 slices sourdough bread
shaved radish, to serve

AVOCADO PUREE

3 avocados, halved and flesh scooped out
50ml buttermilk
juice of 1 lemon
pinch of smoked paprika
pinch of cayenne pepper

METHOD

Combine the crab, mayonnaise, onion, avocado, herbs and spices in a bowl. Season with lemon zest, lemon juice, salt and freshly ground black pepper to taste.

To make the avocado puree, combine all the ingredients in a blender and blend until smooth. Season with salt to taste.

Grill the sourdough bread until golden. Serve topped with the crab mixture, spoonfuls of avocado puree, and the shaved radish.

FRIED BREAD AND RED PEPPER JAM WITH WHITE ANCHOVIES

SERVES 4

INGREDIENTS

RED PEPPER JAM

6 red capsicums

50ml extra virgin olive oil

4 star anise

1 cinnamon stick

100g brown sugar

150ml red wine vinegar

50ml chilli sauce

300g drained bottled red capsicum,
    blended until smooth

FRIED BREAD

50g butter

1 garlic clove, smashed

1 sprig thyme

4 day-old sourdough rolls, split in half

16 white anchovies, to serve

finely grated zest of 1 lemon, to serve

¼ bunch flat-leaf parsley, roughly chopped

METHOD

To make the red pepper jam, char the capsicums over an open flame, turning to cook evenly, until the skin blackens and blisters. Cover with foil or put in a plastic bag to cool and loosen skins. Remove skin, seeds and membrane, and dice the flesh.

Heat the oil in a deep frying pan over medium-low heat, and sweat the diced capsicum with the star anise and cinnamon for about 10 minutes, or until soft.

Add the sugar, vinegar, chilli sauce and blended peppers. Cook over low heat until reduced by half. Season with salt and freshly ground black pepper to taste, and refrigerate to cool completely.

For the fried bread, melt the butter in a frying pan over medium heat, and add the garlic and thyme. Add the rolls cut-side down and cook slowly, until crisp, golden brown and caramelised. Drain and season to taste.

Smear the cooked side of each roll with 1 tablespoon of red pepper jam. Add 4 white anchovies per portion and sprinkle with lemon zest and parsley.

NOTE

Left-over red pepper jam will keep in a jar in the fridge for a few weeks.

CONFIT CHICKEN WINGETTES, CHICKEN PARFAIT AND APPLE CHUTNEY WITH FRIED TORTILLA

SERVES 6

INGREDIENTS

12 chicken wingettes (middle section of the wing)
2 garlic cloves, crushed
¼ bunch thyme
1 litre vegetable oil, plus extra to fry
2 plain flour tortillas, cut into triangles
2 tbsp plain flour
10g butter
1 garlic clove, extra
1 sprig thyme, extra

CHICKEN PARFAIT
500g chicken livers
milk, to soak
300ml port
1 shallot, finely chopped
1 garlic clove, smashed
1 sprig thyme
1 bay leaf
2 eggs, lightly beaten
100g butter, melted and cooled
splash of olive oil

APPLE CHUTNEY
2kg Granny Smith apples
2 tsp salt
1 pinch of cayenne pepper
2 pinches of ground turmeric
50g mustard seeds
1 tsp ground cumin
2 tsp ground ginger
100g fresh ginger, finely grated
2 garlic cloves, finely grated
750ml malt vinegar

600g brown sugar
500g sultanas

METHOD

Place the wingettes into a large dish and add the garlic and thyme. Turn to coat, cover and refrigerate for 12 hours. In preparation for the chicken parfait, place the livers into a bowl, cover with milk and soak overnight in the fridge.

To make the chicken parfait, preheat the oven to 90°C. Combine the port, shallot, garlic, thyme and bay leaf in a small saucepan. Bring to the boil, and cook until reduced to 100ml (one third of original quantity). Cool to room temperature, then remove the thyme and bay leaf.

Blend the drained livers and the port syrup. With the motor running, gradually add the eggs, then the butter.

Lightly oil a 1 litre plastic container with an airtight lid. Pour in the mixture, and seal the lid firmly. Stand the container in a roasting pan, on a flat surface, and add enough warm water to come halfway up the sides. Cook for 30 minutes, or until set with a slight wobble (it will be 60°C if testing with a thermometer). Cool slightly, then refrigerate until chilled and firm.

For the apple chutney, peel, core and roughly chop three quarters of the apples. Place into a colander over a bowl, and sprinkle with the salt. Cover and refrigerate for 1 hour.

Remove the apples from the fridge and squeeze off the excess juice. Heat a large saucepan over medium heat, add the roughly chopped apples and the dry spices and cook for 1 minute. Stir in the fresh ginger, garlic, vinegar and sugar. Increase the heat to high and bring to the boil. Stir continuously until the apples begin to break down, then reduce to a fast simmer and cook until the mixture starts to thicken and slightly change colour.

Meanwhile, peel and core the remaining apples, and cut into 5mm cubes. Add to the pan along with the sultanas, and cook for a further 10 minutes. Cool, then store in an airtight container in the fridge.

Preheat the oven to 90°C. Line a roasting pan with foil and arrange the wingettes in a single layer. Heat the oil slightly, and pour over wings. Cover the baking tray tightly with foil. Cook for 2 hours, until the bones pull out easily, leaving the wingettes still in shape.

While still warm, remove all the bones and lay the wingettes onto a tray lined with baking paper. Top with another sheet of baking paper, and lay another tray on top. Press with a light weight (a couple of cans will do) and refrigerate until cold. Meanwhile, heat 1.5cm vegetable oil in a frying pan over medium heat, and cook the tortilla triangles until golden on both sides. Drain on paper towels.

Dust the skin side of the wingettes with flour, shaking off the excess. Heat a splash of vegetable oil in a large frying pan over medium heat and arrange wingettes skin-side down. Cook slowly until golden. Add the butter, extra garlic and thyme. When the butter has melted, baste the wingettes. Turn and heat through the flesh side for a minute. Serve immediately, with the parfait, chutney and tortillas.

NOTES

When making the parfait, make sure all the ingredients are at room temperature before blending, and add the eggs and butter very slowly. This helps with emulsifying and to avoid the mixture splitting.

Remaining parfait will keep for up to 1 week in the fridge. The apple chutney will keep for up to 3 months in sterilised jars, and once opened, for 6 weeks in the fridge.

CRISPY HAM AND CHEESE BALLS WITH MUSTARD CRÈME FRAÎCHE

MAKES 24

INGREDIENTS
splash of olive oil
2 onions, roughly sliced
2 garlic cloves, chopped
¼ bunch thyme
3 sprigs rosemary
500ml milk
500ml ham hock stock (see Basics, p. 232)
325g unsalted butter
325g plain flour
375g chopped ham hock meat (see Basics, p. 232)
225g grated cheddar
1½ tbsp seeded mustard
1½ tbsp hot English mustard
plain flour, to dust
3 eggs
packaged dry breadcrumbs, to coat
vegetable oil, to deep fry

MUSTARD CRÈME FRAÎCHE
4 tbsp crème fraîche
1 tsp Dijon mustard
1 tsp hot English mustard
juice of ½ lemon

METHOD
Heat the olive oil in a large saucepan and sweat the onion and garlic over medium heat, until soft. Add the herbs, milk and hock stock and bring to the boil. Simmer for a couple of minutes then strain and let cool.

Melt the butter in a separate large saucepan and whisk in the flour. Cook over medium-low heat for 1 minute, making sure it stays blonde. Add the milk mixture gradually, stirring until smooth between each addition. Add the chopped ham and the cheddar, and cook for a further 5 minutes or until the cheese has melted. Stir in the mustards and season with salt and freshly ground black pepper to taste.

Line a 30cm x 20cm x 5cm pan with baking paper. Pour the mixture into the pan, cover with baking paper and refrigerate for 2 hours, or until it has set firmly enough to cut. Cut into 24 even-sized pieces, and shape into balls. Return to the fridge for 1½ hours, or until firm.

Meanwhile, make the mustard crème fraîche. Whisk the ingredients together in a bowl until thick. Season to taste. Cover and refrigerate until serving time.

Set out three bowls. Put the flour into one, whisk the eggs in the second, and put the breadcrumbs into the third. Roll the balls in the flour, dip in the egg, then roll in the breadcrumbs, shaking off the excess each time. Repeat the egg and crumb steps, to give a double coating.

Half fill a large pot with oil (or use a deep-fryer) and heat to 160°C. Fry the balls in batches until golden brown and hot on the inside. Drain on paper towels, and serve immediately with the mustard crème fraîche.

CHEF'S MIDNIGHT SNACK

After a long service late at night, this is the kind of food that sustains us chefs. Garnish heavily with red wine.

SERVES 4

INGREDIENTS
4 slices sourdough bread
4 slices Bûche d'Affinois

ONION JAM
6 onions, finely sliced
180ml extra virgin olive oil
80g butter
80ml port
50ml sherry vinegar

METHOD
To make the onion jam, heat a large saucepan or deep frying pan over high heat. Add the onion then the oil, and cook, stirring, for about 4 minutes or until golden brown.

Reduce heat to low and add the butter. Cook, stirring, for 30 minutes or until darker brown. Add the port and bring to the boil, then stir in the vinegar. Season with salt and freshly ground black pepper, to taste.

To assemble the sandwiches, toast the bread on both sides. Smear with onion jam and place cheese on top. Heat under the grill until soft (but not melted, as it will become too runny). Top with a little more jam, and serve immediately.

NOTE
If you can't get Bûche d'Affinois, use a good brie. You will make enough onion jam for about 4 to 6 sandwiches. Keep left-over onion jam in the fridge for up to 2 weeks.

PORK SCRATCHINGS

The ultimate bar snack. It's crispy, fatty, salty – the essence of pork flavour in a light, crunchy cracker. Best washed down with an ice-cold beer.

SERVES 10

INGREDIENTS

1kg pork skin (fat removed)
100ml white vinegar
10 tbsp table salt
vegetable oil, to deep-fry

METHOD

Place the pork skin into a large pot and cover with water. Stir in the vinegar and table salt. Bring to the boil then reduce the heat to low and simmer, uncovered, for 2 hours. Remove from the heat and cool slightly, then lift out (be careful as it will be delicate and can tear easily) and set aside to cool completely.

Preheat the oven to 95°C. Place a rack into a roasting pan, and line with baking paper. Punch holes into the paper so the fat can drain through. Scrape off any excess fat still on the skin, then place skin side up onto the rack. Cook until the skin becomes crisp and slightly glass-like. It should be crisp enough to snap, and not bend or tear. Cool and break into pieces.

Half fill a large pot with oil (or use a deep-fryer) and heat to 200°C. Test by dropping a piece of pork skin into the oil – it should expand and bubble within a few seconds. Cook the skin in batches, turning to ensure even cooking. Drain on paper towels, and season with sea salt.

BEER-BATTERED ONION RINGS

SERVES 10

INGREDIENTS
vegetable oil, to deep-fry
5 onions, cut into 3cm-thick rings
plain flour, to dust

BEER BATTER
10g fresh yeast
300ml beer
100g plain flour
80g rice flour
20g cornflour
10g salt

METHOD
To make the beer batter, dissolve the yeast in a little of the beer, then stir in the remaining beer. Sift the flours and salt into a bowl and make a well in the centre. Gradually add the beer, stirring to combine. Set aside to rest for at least 1 hour.

Half fill a large pot with oil (or use a deep-fryer) and heat to 180°C. Dust the onions lightly with flour, and shake off excess. Working in batches, dip onions into the batter. Fry until crisp and golden. Drain on paper towels and season with salt. Repeat with remaining onions, and serve immediately.

PORK SCRATCHINGS

BEER–BATTERED ONION RINGS

PORK POPCORN

SERVES LOTS

INGREDIENTS
splash of vegetable oil
150g popping corn kernels
1 chorizo, finely sliced
2 star anise
1 cinnamon stick
1 sprig rosemary
pinch of cayenne pepper
pinch of smoked paprika

METHOD
Heat the oil in a large pot over high heat. Add the popping corn, and stir until it just starts to pop. Stir in remaining ingredients and cover with a lid.

Keep cooking until the popping sounds slow right down. Remove from the heat, uncover and season with salt, stirring to mix through.

OYSTERS AND PICKLED SEAWEED

When oysters are at their best, serve them simply and let them do the talking.

SERVES 6

INGREDIENTS
100g dried wakame seaweed
pickling liquor (see p. 173)
24 Clair de Lune oysters
4 lemons, quartered

METHOD
Place the seaweed into hot pickling liquor and leave for 1 hour to soak and cool. Drain.

Just before serving, open the oysters, and replace lids loosely. Place the oysters on stones (see Note).

Garnish with the soaked seaweed, and serve with lemon on the side.

NOTE
We use chilled stones to serve the oysters on, but you could use rock salt, if you like.

ENTRÉES

Entrées are the traditional start to the meal and your first shot at the title. I find that I can showcase more skill in entrées because they're a lot smaller, which means you can play around with flavours and textures and be more intricate in plating up.

Entrées are the essence of a dish, without filling you up: all killer, no filler here.

These recipes are a mixture of rustic and fine, but what links them is that flavour is the most important element. In a restaurant sense, we're trying to hook you in, and when you're cooking for friends at home you should try to do the same.

A good entrée should relax you and get you excited about what's to come. In a date sense, this is where you get to hold hands.

MUSHROOM TEA

SERVES 4

INGREDIENTS

30g mixed dried mushrooms
200ml port
splash of olive oil
1 onion, chopped
2 garlic cloves, chopped
300g button mushrooms, chopped
80g king brown mushrooms, sliced
80g Swiss brown mushrooms, sliced

METHOD

Place the dried mushrooms into a bowl and add the port. Soak for 30 minutes.

Heat the oil in a saucepan over low heat, and sweat the onion and garlic until soft. Add the button mushrooms and sweat for 1 minute. Drain the dried mushrooms, reserving the port. Squeeze out excess liquid back into the bowl. Add soaked mushrooms to the pan and sweat for 1 minute.

Deglaze pan with the reserved port. Add 1.5 litres water to the pan, bring to the boil then remove from the heat. Cover the saucepan with a lid and leave to sit for 45 minutes.

Strain the broth into a saucepan, add the king brown and Swiss brown mushrooms and reheat gently. Sit for 5 minutes, then season with salt and freshly ground black pepper and serve.

EEL MOUSSE

SERVES 4

INGREDIENTS

250g cream cheese, at room temperature, chopped
1 side of smoked eel, skinned and boned
Finely grated lemon zest and juice, to taste
150ml cream
shaved baby beetroot (use different colours)
Finely grated fresh horseradish, to serve

METHOD

Combine the cream cheese and eel in a blender, and blend until smooth. Add zest and juice to taste.

Whip cream until soft peaks form, and fold through the eel mixture. Season with salt and freshly ground black pepper to taste, and chill for 1 hour.

Serve the mousse with shaved beets and horseradish.

NOTE

Use a microplane to grate horseradish directly over plates.

BRAISED PIG'S TAIL

The essence of Four in Hand on a plate. It's rough and elegant at the same time and takes the philosophy of nose-to-tail eating literally. It's my Irish version of surf and turf.

SERVES 4

INGREDIENTS
splash of olive oil
1 carrot, roughly chopped
1 onion, roughly chopped
2 celery stalks, roughly chopped
2 garlic cloves, crushed
200ml port
4 pigs' tails
600ml chicken stock
1 bay leaf

PRAWN BISQUE
500g prawn shells
2 onions, roughly chopped
2 carrots, roughly chopped
1 celery stalk, roughly chopped
200ml white wine
3 star anise
2 lemongrass stalks, bruised
50g ginger, chopped
2 kaffir lime leaves
250g canned diced tomatoes
2 litres fish stock
200ml cream
finely grated zest and juice of 2 lemons

CRAB AND CORN SALAD
300g picked Alaskan King or Blue Swimmer crab meat
3 corn cobs
splash of olive oil
1 garlic clove, smashed
1 sprig thyme
1 sprig rosemary
¼ bunch parsley, leaves roughly chopped
80ml vierge dressing [see Basics, p. 227]

AVOCADO PUREE
3 avocados, halved and flesh scooped out
50ml buttermilk
juice of 1 lemon
pinch of smoked paprika
pinch of cayenne pepper

METHOD
Preheat the oven to 150°C. Heat the oil in a large flameproof casserole over medium heat, and add the vegetables and garlic. Sweat down until soft. Add the port and bring to the boil. Add the pigs' tails, chicken stock and bay leaf. Bring to the boil.

Cover with a lid (or baking paper and foil) and bake for about 4 hours or until tender. Cool slightly, then drain off the stock. Carefully pull out the bones.

Meanwhile, for the prawn bisque, preheat the oven to 200°C. Working in 3 batches, spread the prawn shells on an oven tray and roast for about 20 minutes, stirring often, until golden. Place two thirds of the roasted shells into a large saucepan with the chopped vegetables, white wine, star anise and half the lemongrass, ginger and lime leaves. Bring to the boil.

Add the tomatoes, stock and cream. Bring to the boil, reduce the heat to low and simmer for 40 minutes, skimming the surface occasionally. Strain, and return to the pan. Add the reserved shells, lemongrass, ginger and lime leaves and simmer for 5 minutes. Strain again. Add the lemon zest and juice, and season with salt and freshly ground black pepper, to taste.

To make the crab and corn salad, pick any shell out of the crab meat and keep in the fridge until needed. Cut the kernels from the corn cobs. Heat the oil in a frying pan (with a lid ready to use close by).

Add the corn kernels, garlic and herbs. Give a quick stir then put the lid on. Cook for a few minutes then stir again. Be careful, as it might spit at this stage. Continue to cook for about 6–8 minutes, until the corn is golden and has a soft bite. Remove from the pan and set aside to cool before using. Combine the corn and crab meat. Dress with vierge dressing, and season with salt and freshly ground black pepper.

For the avocado puree, combine all the ingredients in a blender and mix until smooth. Season to taste.

To serve, spoon a bed of crab and corn salad onto plates, and top with a pigs' tail. Add a quenelle of avocado puree, and serve with prawn bisque on the side.

TUNA, LEMON CURD AND CUCUMBER JUICE

SERVES 6

INGREDIENTS
360g sashimi-grade tuna
4cm knob of ginger
splash of soy dressing (see Basics, p. 226)
120g pickled wakame (see p. 28)
shredded nori, to serve
shisho and samphire, to garnish

LEMON CURD
2 lemons, scrubbed
75g butter, chopped
25g sugar

CUCUMBER JUICE
1 cucumber, chopped (skin on)
3g ginger, chopped
5 English spinach leaves, chopped
175ml ginger beer
splash of lemon juice

METHOD
To make the lemon curd, place the whole lemons into a large saucepan and cover with water. Bring to the boil, then reduce the heat and simmer for 30 minutes or until very soft.

Lift lemons from the pan and cool slightly. Reserve 100ml of the cooking liquid. Cut lemons in half and discard the pips. Place into a blender with the reserved cooking liquid and blend until smooth. Add the butter and blend until combined. Stir in the sugar, and season with salt, to taste.

For the cucumber juice, combine the ingredients in a blender and blend until smooth (do not allow to get warm). Strain, then chill over ice and season with salt, to taste.

Cut the tuna into 1cm cubes, and spread onto a plate in a single layer. Finely grate the ginger over the tuna and drizzle with a little soy dressing. Leave to marinate at room temperature for 30 minutes.

To serve, arrange the tuna and wakame onto plates. Dot with lemon curd, sprinkle with nori, shisho and samphire, and pour cucumber juice over.

NOTE
Cucumber juice can be made ahead of time and kept in the fridge, but use within 24 hours of making. Keep left-over lemon curd in the fridge for up to 1 week.

SUMMER MELON WITH HAM AND MELON GRANITA

SERVES 6

INGREDIENTS

MELON GRANITA

1 rockmelon
1 litre sugar syrup (see Basics, p. 233)
1½ tsp salt
juice of 1 lemon

TO SERVE

cubed rockmelon, watermelon, honeydew melon
    and cucumber
120g shaved ham (I use Kurobuta ham)
handful small mint leaves

METHOD

To make the melon granita, cut open the melon, remove the skin and scoop out the seeds. Roughly chop the flesh and put into a blender with the remaining ingredients. Blend until smooth, then pass through a strainer. Pour the mixture into a chilled metal tray and freeze for 1 hour, or until solid.

To serve, arrange melon and cucumber cubes onto plates. Add ham and mint leaves. Use a fork to scrape the frozen mixture into crystals, and sprinkle over the plates. Serve immediately.

MISO-MARINATED SMOKED KING SALMON

One of the original and best menu items from 4Fourteen, and it's all about umami. This dish is a real crowd-pleaser.

SERVES 4

INGREDIENTS

50ml soy sauce
½ stalk lemongrass
1 kaffir lime leaf
60g fresh ginger
5 coriander seeds
250g smoked King salmon fillet, cut into four slices
150g light miso paste
fennel lavosh, to serve (see p. 200)
pickled cauliflower (see method p. 173), to serve
cucumber ribbons and shaved radishes, to serve

MISO MAYONNAISE

400g mayonnaise (see Basics, p. 233)
200g light miso paste
fresh finely grated horseradish, to taste
finely grated lemon zest and juice, to taste

METHOD

Combine the soy sauce and 300ml water in a medium saucepan. Bash the lemongrass with a rolling pin to bruise and slit it, releasing the flavour. Bruise the lime leaf and roughly chop the ginger.

Toast the coriander seeds in a dry frying pan for 1 minute. Add to the saucepan with the lemongrass, lime leaf and ginger. Bring to the boil, and cook for 3 minutes. Remove from the heat and leave to cool.

Place the salmon slices into a glass or ceramic shallow dish. Whisk the miso paste into the cold soy mixture, and pour over the salmon. Cover and refrigerate for 24 hours.

To make the miso mayonnaise, mix the mayonnaise and miso together, and add horseradish, lemon zest and juice to taste. Season with salt.

Heat a large heavy-based frying pan over high heat. Drain the marinade from the salmon, and add the salmon to the pan. Cook one side for about 20 seconds, until golden and caramelised.

Serve the salmon between pieces of fennel lavosh with pickled cauliflower, cucumber ribbons, shaved radishes and miso mayonnaise.

ARTICHOKE AND CHEESE RIND SOUP

This dish brings me back to my days of working with Raymond Blanc. I was 24, tired, skinny and starving, but the beauty and earthiness of artichokes struck a chord with me and I've loved them ever since.

SERVES 6

INGREDIENTS
500g Jerusalem artichokes
splash of olive oil
1 onion, chopped
3 garlic cloves, chopped
500ml white wine
100g parmesan rind
300ml chicken stock
200ml cream
lemon juice, to taste
splash extra virgin olive oil
freshly grated parmesan, to serve

ARTICHOKE CHIPS
1 Jerusalem artichoke, finely sliced
vegetable oil, to deep fry

METHOD
Peel and chop the artichokes. Heat the oil in a medium-large saucepan and add the onion and garlic. Sweat over medium-low heat until soft but not coloured, then add the artichokes.

Add the wine and bring to the boil. Add the rind, stock and cream. Bring to a simmer and cook for 30 minutes or until very soft. Stir in the lemon juice. Remove rind.

Blend the mixture until smooth, and pass through a fine sieve into a clean saucepan. Reheat gently and season with salt to taste. Serve drizzled with extra virgin olive oil, grated parmesan and artichoke chips.

To make the artichoke chips, half fill a pan with oil (or use a deep-fryer) and heat to 140°C. Deep-fry the artichoke slices until golden and crisp. Drain on paper towel.

SPLIT PEA AND ISRAELI COUSCOUS SOUP

SERVES 8

INGREDIENTS

splash of olive oil

1 carrot, diced

1 onion, diced

1 celery, sliced

3 garlic cloves, chopped

100ml white wine

200g Israeli couscous

300g green split peas

2 litres vegetable stock (plus more if you like)

thyme leaves, to serve

METHOD

Heat the oil in a large saucepan over low heat. Add the vegetables and garlic, and sweat until soft but not coloured. Deglaze with white wine then add the couscous.

Add the split peas and stock. Bring to the boil then reduce the heat slightly and cook uncovered for 30 minutes or until the vegetables, couscous and peas are tender. Add more stock as it cooks if you like, but it is supposed to be a thick and chunky soup.

Season with salt and freshly ground black pepper, and serve sprinkled with thyme leaves.

NOTE

This soup is suitable to freeze.

ARTICHOKE AND CHEESE RIND SOUP

ROAST LIVE SCALLOP AND SEAWEED

SERVES 4

INGREDIENTS
16 Rottnest Island live scallops
splash of olive oil
finely grated fresh horseradish, to serve
finely grated lemon zest, to serve
pickled seaweed (see p. 28)
lemon juice, to taste

METHOD
Open the scallops and loosen from the shells. Remove skirt, and rinse. Add a little olive oil to each scallop, then replace lids. Roast over glowing coals for 3 minutes, turn and rest off the heat for 1 minute. Alternatively, cook under a hot grill for the same amount of time.

Open the scallops and top with horseradish and lemon zest. Serve with pickled seaweed and lemon juice.

NOTE
Use a microplane to grate horseradish and zest directly over scallops.

WHOLE ROAST MISO CORN

SERVES 4

INGREDIENTS
4 corn cobs (in husks)
100g unsalted butter, softened
100g white miso paste
3cm knob of ginger, grated
juice of 2 limes

METHOD
Preheat a BBQ or chargrill to hot. Cook the corn for about 5 minutes, turning regularly, until they begin to blacken.

Meanwhile, use an electric mixer to beat the remaining ingredients until well combined. Transfer to a large bowl.

Remove the husks from the corn cobs, and while still hot toss through the miso mixture to coat.

PIG'S EARS

This is one of the first dishes I came up with at the Four in Hand. It's still around in some form today and I love the contrast of textures: crispy on the outside and soft and a little crunchy on the inside, all in one bite.

SERVES 6

INGREDIENTS
splash of olive oil
1 carrot, roughly chopped
1 onion, roughly chopped
2 celery stalks, roughly chopped
2 garlic cloves, crushed
200ml port
3cm knob of ginger, roughly chopped
1 star anise
1 cinnamon stick
1 bay leaf
6 pigs' ears
600ml chicken stock
plain flour, to dust
2 eggs, lightly beaten
2 tbsp milk
dry packaged breadcrumbs, to coat
vegetable oil, to deep fry
sage salt, to taste (see p. 226)

SALSA VERDE
½ bunch parsley
½ bunch basil
½ bunch mint
100ml red wine vinegar
100ml olive oil
50g cornichons
50g capers
1 tbsp mustard

METHOD
Preheat the oven to 90°C. Heat the oil in a flameproof casserole over medium heat, and add the vegetables and garlic. Sweat down until soft. Add the port and bring to the boil. Add the ginger, star anise, cinnamon, bay leaf, pigs' ears and chicken stock. Bring to the boil. Cover and place into the oven for 12 hours.

Lift the pigs' ears from the pan. Place onto a tray, top with another tray and weigh down with 1kg weight (you can use cans as weights). Refrigerate for 2 hours, until cold and set.

To make the salsa verde, combine all the ingredients in a blender and blend until smooth.

Set out three bowls. Put the flour into one, whisk the eggs and milk in the second, and put the breadcrumbs into the third. Coat the ears in the flour, then the eggs and milk, and then the breadcrumbs, shaking off the excess each time.

Half fill a large pot with vegetable oil (or use a deep-fryer) and heat to 160°C. Deep-fry the ears in batches for 3–4 minutes or until golden brown. Drain on paper towels. Serve immediately with salsa verde and sage salt.

NOTE
Salsa verde can be kept in the fridge for up to 5 days.

SMOKED HAM HOCK TERRINE AND PICCALILLI

SERVES 10

INGREDIENTS

PICCALILLI (MAKES ABOUT 9 CUPS)
2kg vegetables (see Note)
100g table salt
1 litre cider vinegar
60g cornflour
20g turmeric
20g English mustard powder
20g ground ginger
1 tbsp mustard seeds
2 tbsp crushed cumin seeds
2 tbsp crushed coriander seeds
400g sugar
10g honey

TERRINE
4 smoked ham hocks
1 onion, diced
2 celery stalks, diced
2 carrots, whole
1 bay leaf
¼ bunch thyme
¼ bunch rosemary
3 litres cider
100g cornichons, finely chopped
60g baby salted capers, rinsed,
   drained and finely chopped
1 bunch flat-leaf parsley, leaves roughly chopped
20ml sherry vinegar
finely grated zest and juice of 1 lemon

METHOD

To make the piccalilli, cut the vegetables into bite-sized pieces, and place into a glass or ceramic bowl. Sprinkle with salt, and refrigerate for 24 hours. Rinse in a colander under cold running water.

Mix 200ml of the vinegar with the cornflour and spices. Combine the remaining vinegar with the sugar and honey in a saucepan. Stir over low heat to dissolve the sugar, then add the cornflour mixture and bring to the boil. Cook for 4–5 minutes.

Pour the liquid over the vegetables, and put into sterilised jars. Seal tightly, and store in a cool, dark place for 6 weeks before eating. Store in the fridge for up to 1 week after opening. Unopened jars will keep for up to 6 months.

For the terrine, combine the hocks, vegetables, bay leaf, thyme and rosemary in a large pot. Cover with the cider. Bring to the boil then reduce the heat and simmer, covered, for about 3 hours, or until the meat is falling off the bone. Let the hocks cool in the stock. Lift out and pick the meat off. Discard the bones.

Strain the stock through a fine strainer into a clean saucepan. Bring to the boil, reduce the heat slightly and cook until reduced by half. Return the hock meat to the vegetables, and discard the bay leaf and any coarse herb stems.

Fold the cornichons, capers and parsley through the mixture. Add the vinegar, lemon zest and juice, and stock. Season to taste.

Line a 2.5 litre capacity terrine or loaf tin with cling wrap. Fill with terrine mix, pressing in firmly with the back of a spoon. Cover top with cling wrap and place another dish the same size on top. Press with a weight (about 2 kg), and refrigerate overnight, until set.

Cut terrine into slices, and serve with piccalilli.

NOTE
For the piccalilli, use vegetables such as cauliflower, pearl onions, carrots, green beans, cucumber, radish and eggplant.

HEIRLOOM TOMATOES, BUTTERMILK CURD AND TOMATO WATER

SERVES 4-6

INGREDIENTS

1kg mixed heirloom tomatoes, sliced
vierge dressing (see Basics, p. 227)
micro basil leaves, to serve

BUTTERMILK CURD

600ml carton buttermilk
200g natural yoghurt
100ml extra virgin olive oil
finely grated zest and juice of 1 lemon
pinch of salt

TOMATO WATER

1kg ripe tomatoes, chopped
1 red onion, chopped
2 garlic cloves, chopped
200ml white wine
2 bay leaves
½ bunch basil, leaves picked
½ bunch tarragon, leaves picked
1 tsp Worcestershire sauce
200g sugar
lemon juice, to taste

CROUTONS

1 sourdough roll (day-old is best)
olive oil

METHOD

To make the buttermilk curd, place the buttermilk carton into a saucepan. Add enough water to come right up to the top. Slowly bring to a simmer over low heat. Simmer for 30 minutes, remove from pan and allow to cool in carton.

When cold, strain the resulting curd through a fine sieve. Whisk the yoghurt, oil, lemon zest and juice, and salt into the curd.

To make the tomato water, combine the tomatoes, onion and garlic in a small saucepan. Add the wine and bring to the boil. Cover with water and add the bay leaves. Bring to a simmer, and cook for 20 minutes. Tear the basil and tarragon leaves and add to the pan, followed by the Worcestershire sauce and sugar.

Line a colander with a clean tea towel and stand over a deep bowl. Pour the mixture into the tea towel, and leave to strain slowly for about 3 hours (the strained water should be clear). Place in the fridge to chill. Season and add lemon juice, to taste.

To make the croutons, preheat the oven to 180°C. Thinly slice the roll into wafers, and arrange in a single layer on a baking tray. Brush with olive oil and season with salt and freshly ground black pepper. Bake until golden brown. Cool completely, then store in an airtight container if not using immediately.

To serve, arrange sliced tomatoes into shallow dishes. Pour the tomato water over, and dot with buttermilk curd. Drizzle with vierge dressing and sprinkle with croutons and micro basil leaves.

NOTE

Keep left-over curd in the fridge for up to 1 week.

CRAB, FENNEL CUSTARD, CONFIT FENNEL AND HAZELNUTS

SERVES 6

INGREDIENTS

300g cooked, picked Alaskan King crab
50g hazelnuts, roasted, skinned and finely chopped

FENNEL CUSTARD

splash of extra virgin oil
1 onion, diced
2 garlic cloves, chopped
2 fennel bulbs, chopped (keep fronds for garnish)
1 star anise
5g fennel seeds, lightly toasted
100ml white wine vinegar
500ml cream
12 egg yolks

CONFIT FENNEL

1 fennel bulb, cut into 1cm dice
sugar syrup (see Basics, p. 233)
30ml pernod
splash of lemon juice

METHOD

To make the fennel custard, preheat the oven to 90°C. Heat the oil in a saucepan. Sweat the onion, garlic and fennel over low heat until soft but not coloured. Add the star anise and fennel seeds and cook, stirring, for 2 minutes. Add the wine and bring to the boil, then stir in the cream.

Allow the mixture to cool completely, then remove the star anise. Blend until smooth and pass through a fine sieve. Whisk the egg yolks in a bowl. Reheat the cream mixture, and gradually add to the yolks, whisking constantly. Pass through a fine sieve again.

Line a 15cm x 10cm x 5cm ovenproof dish with cling wrap. Pour in the custard, and cover the top with cling wrap. Line a roasting pan with a folded tea towel, and stand the dish on it. Add enough warm water to come halfway up the sides. Cook for 35 minutes, or until it has a slight wobble (it will be 80°C in the centre if testing with a thermometer). Cool in the fridge. When cold, pour into a bowl and whisk. Taste and season if necessary.

For the confit fennel, place the fennel into a saucepan, and cover with sugar syrup. Season with salt and freshly ground black pepper, and add the pernod. Cook over low heat for 5 minutes, until just soft. Add the lemon juice and allow to cool completely.

To serve, spoon fennel custard into shallow dishes. Arrange the confit fennel over and around, and top with crab meat. Sprinkle with hazelnuts, and garnish with reserved fennel fronds.

CHICKEN LIVERS WITH SHERRY VINEGAR, PROSCIUTTO AND ONION JAM

SERVES 4 (OR 2 AS A MAIN)

INGREDIENTS
splash of olive oil
100g cleaned chicken livers
15g butter
2 sprigs thyme
2 garlic cloves, crushed
100ml sherry vinegar

TO SERVE
onion jam (see p. 20)
finely shaved prosciutto
chicken parfait (see p. 16)
watercress
sourdough bread

METHOD
Heat the oil in a frying pan over high heat. Add the livers and cook for about 1 minute, until lightly browned, but still pink in the middle.

Add the butter, thyme and garlic. Baste the livers until the butter is golden. Deglaze with sherry vinegar, then drain the livers on paper towel.

Serve immediately with the onion jam, prosciutto, chicken parfait, watercress and sourdough bread.

FENNEL POPSICLES

This is a clever way to incorporate vegetables, particularly fennel, into a dish. It's also a cunning way to get my kids to eat green vegetables! Works well with the fennel custard dish.

MAKES 10

INGREDIENTS

2 fennel bulbs, with fronds, roughly chopped
600ml carton buttermilk
150g liquid glucose
4 leaves English spinach
lemon juice, to taste

METHOD

Put the fennel, buttermilk, glucose and spinach into a blender and blend until smooth. Strain through a sieve, and season with lemon juice and salt, to taste.

Pour into ten 150ml popsicle moulds. Place into the freezer, and once they start to freeze put wooden sticks into the mixture. Freeze until firm.

MEAT AND POULTRY

Welcome to my world.

After years of trying to master the art of cooking meat, I've learnt that meat can be gentle and subtle. Meat, and the way you cook it, is all about your own preference, but it's also about science. Roasting, braising, poaching, frying, coaxing maximum flavours and textures ... they all require a bit of time and patience, and for mistakes to be made. Also, don't underestimate the power of secondary cuts – if you eat meat, you should respect the whole beast by learning how to cook from all of it. Secondary cuts in my eyes are actually primary – they often have more flavour and you can create some really spectacular things with them.

CORNED BEEF AND SPRING SOUP WITH DUMPLINGS

SERVES 6

INGREDIENTS
STOCK
1kg piece corned beef
1 onion, roughly chopped
1 carrot, roughly chopped
1 celery stalk, roughly chopped
1 garlic bulb, smashed
1 bay leaf
½ bunch thyme
½ bunch rosemary
1 cinnamon stick
1 star anise
pinch of fennel seeds

SOUP
splash of olive oil
1 onion, diced
1 large carrot, diced
2 celery stalks, diced
1 zucchini, diced
1 fennel bulb, diced
100ml white wine
100ml port
reserved diced meat
handful of peas
1 cup broadbeans
10g basil leaves, torn
10g tarragon leaves, torn
10g marjoram leaves, torn
10g flat-leaf parsley leaves, torn
splash of extra virgin olive oil
lemon juice, to taste

DUMPLINGS
300g self-raising flour
50g fresh herb leaves, such as marjoram, thyme and
    tarragon, chopped
20g finely grated horseradish
salt and freshly ground black pepper

METHOD
For the stock, place all the ingredients into a large pot and cover with water. Bring to a simmer and cook over low heat, covered, for 3 hours, until tender. Leave to cool. When cold, remove the meat and strain the stock. Dice the meat and reserve.

To make the soup, heat the oil in a large saucepan, add the onion, carrot, celery, zucchini and fennel. Sweat over medium-low heat until soft but not coloured.

Add the white wine and port, and bring to the boil. Add 2 litres of the stock, and heat over medium heat without boiling. At the last minute, add the diced meat, peas, broadbeans, herbs, extra virgin olive oil and lemon juice. Heat through, taste and season if necessary.

Meanwhile, make the dumplings. Combine the flour, herbs and horseradish with salt and freshly ground black pepper in a large bowl. Mix in enough warm water to make a soft dough. Gather the dough together and mould into small balls (about thumbnail size).

Line a large steamer with baking paper. Place the dumplings onto the paper, leaving room in between for rising. Cover and steam over boiling water for 8 minutes.

To serve, divide the dumplings among serving bowls and ladle the soup over.

BEEF AND BONE

SERVES 2

INGREDIENTS

BONE MARROW
1 piece of bone marrow, halved lengthways
1 ½cm piece fresh horseradish, grated

3-HOUR ROAST CARROTS
splash of olive oil
3 carrots, unpeeled
500g cold unsalted butter, diced
4 sprigs thyme
2 garlic cloves, smashed

CELERIAC REMOULADE
1 large celeriac, coarsely grated
100g mayonnaise (see Basics, p. 233)
25g cornichons, finely chopped
25g capers, finely chopped
¼ bunch parsley, leaves roughly chopped
finely grated zest and juice of 1 lemon

BAVETTE
splash of olive oil
450g bavette
20g butter
2 garlic cloves, smashed
4 sprigs of thyme

METHOD

To prepare the bone marrow, trim the excess meaty pieces from the outside of the bone for neat presentation. Run the marrow under cold water to remove the blood. Place into a bowl of iced water in the fridge for 24 hours, changing the water a few times.

For the 3-hour roast carrots, preheat oven to 120°C. Heat the oil in a roasting pan on the stove. Add the carrots and cook over medium heat for about 20 minutes, turning occasionally, to give an even colour. Season with salt and freshly ground black pepper. Add 250g of the butter to the pan and place in oven. When the butter browns, add the remaining butter. Cook for 1½ hours, turning every 20 minutes. Add thyme and garlic, and cook for a further 1½ hours. Keep turning. Remove from oven and cover with foil to keep warm.

To make the celeriac remoulade, sprinkle the celeriac with salt and let it sit for 30 minutes. Squeeze out excess moisture. Combine the celeriac with the mayonnaise, cornichons, capers and parsley. Season with freshly ground black pepper, lemon zest and juice. Should be okay for salt because of previous salting, but check.

To cook the bone marrow, increase the oven temperature to 200°C. Place the marrow into a roasting pan and roast for 5 minutes or until the hard marrow becomes translucent and jelly-like (leave the oven on). Season with salt and grated horseradish. Set aside while you cook the bavette.

For the bavette, heat a splash of oil in a frying pan over high heat. Season the meat with salt and freshly ground black pepper. Seal the meat until golden on both sides. Add the butter, garlic and thyme. Place into the oven and cook for 2 minutes on each side. Remove from the pan and rest for 5 minutes before slicing across the grain. Serve the bone marrow, roast carrots and bavette with the celeriac remoulade on the side.

DUCK BREAST WITH SMOKED PINEAPPLE, PEKING DUCK DICE AND SORBET

SERVES 4

INGREDIENTS
1 celery stalk, finely sliced
splash of vierge dressing (see Basics, p. 227)
baby shiso (Japanese herb) leaves

SORBET
½ Peking duck
40g ginger, chopped
½ garlic bulb, smashed
1 onion, chopped
4 star anise
1 cinnamon stick
300ml soy sauce
100ml fish sauce
4 kaffir lime leaves
1 tbsp liquid glucose

SMOKED PINEAPPLE
200g butter
1 pineapple
1 cinnamon stick, broken
2 star anise
½ handful hickory woodchips

DUCK BREAST
175g salt
175g sugar
2 garlic cloves, smashed
1 bay leaf
5 sprigs thyme
3 star anise
1 cinnamon quill
10 black peppercorns
10 coriander seeds
2 x 200g duck breast fillets
10g butter

METHOD
To make the sorbet, preheat the oven to 180°C. Take the skin from the Peking duck and pull off the meat. Cover and refrigerate the skin and meat until needed. Chop the bones, and place two thirds of them into a roasting pan. Reserve remaining bones. Roast for 10 minutes, until golden. Add the ginger, garlic, onion, star anise and cinnamon, and roast for a further 5 minutes, until brown.

Transfer to a large saucepan, and add the soy sauce, fish sauce, lime leaves, glucose and 1 litre of water. Bring to a simmer, and cook, uncovered, for 1 hour. Strain and add reserved bones. Stand for 5 minutes, then strain again. Cool the liquid, then refrigerate until chilled. Churn in an ice-cream churn according to manufacturer's instructions. Transfer to an airtight container and freeze.

To make the smoked pineapple, preheat the oven to 180°C. Soften the butter and brush over pineapple. Lay out a sheet of foil large enough to wrap pineapple, and put the cinnamon and star anise on it. Place the buttered pineapple on top and wrap the foil tightly around it. Bake for 2 hours. Unwrap and cool slightly.

Heat the woodchips in a cast-iron pan over high heat until smoke rises. Place a wire rack over the pan, and place pineapple on top. Cover pineapple with a large bowl, and smoke for 5 minutes. Remove and cool, then peel and slice.

For the duck breast, bring 1 litre of water to the boil in a saucepan. Add the salt, sugar, garlic, herbs and spices, reduce the heat to low and simmer for 5 minutes. Remove from heat, transfer to a bowl and cool completely. Add the duck breast to the brine mixture, and refrigerate for 2 hours.

Preheat the oven to 180°C. Remove the duck from the brine and pat dry with paper towels. Lightly score the skin to allow the fat to render while cooking. Place the duck, skin-side down, into a cold ovenproof frying pan. Place over medium heat and cook for 10 minutes or until skin becomes crisp.

Place pan in the oven for 4 minutes. Remove from the oven, turn duck skin-side up, add the butter and return to the oven for another minute. Set aside to rest in the pan for 1 minute. Remove from pan, sit for a further 2 minutes, then slice lengthways.

Reduce oven to 150°C. Scrape the fat from the reserved Peking duck skin, and season with salt. Place between 2 sheets of greaseproof paper. Roast for 8–10 minutes, or until crisp. Dice the Peking duck meat.

Serve the sliced duck breast with the diced Peking duck meat, finely sliced celery and smoked pineapple. Dress lightly with vierge dressing, top with a quenelle of sorbet, and sprinkle with shiso leaves.

WALLABY WITH WILD GARLIC

SERVES 4

INGREDIENTS

12 wallaby tenderloins
splash of olive oil
20g butter
2 garlic cloves, smashed
2 sprigs of thyme
blanched wild garlic, to serve
steamed broccoli leaves, to serve

GARLIC PUREE

20ml vegetable oil
½ onion, finely sliced
250g garlic, peeled and finely sliced
50ml white wine vinegar
150ml cream
2 sprigs thyme
juice of 1 lemon

METHOD

To make the garlic puree, heat the oil in a frying pan and sauté the onion and garlic over medium heat until soft but not browned. Add the vinegar, increase the heat and bring to the boil.

Reduce the heat to medium, add the cream and thyme. Cover and cook for 30 minutes. Remove the thyme, add the lemon juice and blend to a puree.

Season the meat with salt and freshly ground black pepper, and heat the oil in a large frying pan over high heat. Add the meat and cook for 30 seconds each side. Reduce the heat to low, add the butter, garlic and thyme, and cook until the butter is brown.

Remove the meat from the pan and rest it for 2 minutes. Gently reheat the garlic puree. Cut the tenderloins into slices. Serve with garlic puree, blanched wild garlic and steamed broccoli leaves.

NOTE

Wallaby tenderloins are produced by Flinders Island Meats. Ask a good butcher, or check their website for details. Left-over garlic puree will keep for up to a week in the fridge.

VEAL WITH POLENTA AND CRISP CHARD

SERVES 6

INGREDIENTS

1 ½ litres milk

1 onion, peeled

½ garlic bulb, smashed

1 bay leaf

½ bunch thyme

100 g parmesan rind, microplaned

1kg veal fillet, trimmed

CRISP CHARD

150g corn flour

150g rice flour

150g plain flour

2 egg yolks, lightly beaten

soda water

vegetable oil, to deep-fry

4 large chard leaves

POLENTA

20g butter

1 onion, chopped

2 garlic cloves, chopped

100ml white wine

100g parmesan rind

300g fine polenta

1 ½ litre reserved veal milk, warmed

Freshly grated parmesan, to serve

METHOD

Combine the milk, onion, garlic, herbs and parmesan rind in a large saucepan, and bring to a simmer. Cook for 5 minutes, then season with salt and freshly ground black pepper and remove from the heat. Sit for 5 minutes, then add the veal. Cover with milk, and heat gently until it comes to 48°C. Remove from the heat, and remove the veal. Strain the milk and reserve for the polenta.

For the crisp chard, sift the flours into a large bowl, season with salt and freshly ground black pepper, and make a well in the centre. Add the egg yolks and gently mix in enough soda water to make a thin batter (the consistency of milk). Half fill a saucepan with oil and heat to 160°C. Dip the chard leaves into the batter and let the excess drain off. Deep-fry until crisp, then drain on paper towels. Break into pieces and season with salt.

To make the polenta, melt the butter in a saucepan, and sweat the onion and garlic over low heat until soft but not coloured. Deglaze with the white wine. Add the rind and polenta. Warm the reserved milk, and gradually add to the pan, stirring constantly. Cook, stirring, for about 30 minutes, or until thickened and very soft (it shouldn't be grainy at all).

To serve, slice the veal, and serve with the polenta and crisp chard. Sprinkle parmesan over the polenta.

NOTE

You can use kale leaves instead of chard if you like.

MY CHICKEN SOUP

SERVES 4

INGREDIENTS
splash of olive oil
1 carrot, diced
1 onion, diced
1 celery stalk, diced
2 garlic cloves, diced
200ml white wine
1 bay leaf
3 sprigs of thyme
2 ½ litres chicken stock
4 chicken marylands
100g pearl barley
2 large kale leaves, ripped
lemon juice, to taste
extra virgin olive oil, to finish

METHOD
Heat the oil in a large saucepan, and sweat the vegetables and garlic over medium heat, until soft. Deglaze with white wine and bring to the boil.

Add the herbs, stock and chicken. Bring to a simmer, and cook uncovered for 1 hour, until the meat is falling off the bone. Lift the chicken from the pot, cool slightly and take the meat from the bones (discard the skin). Return the meat to the soup.

Meanwhile, place the barley into a sieve and rinse under cold running water. Place into a saucepan, cover with cold water, and bring to the boil. Reduce the heat slightly and simmer for 10 minutes or until just cooked. Drain and refresh in cold water; drain again.

Reheat the soup and stir in the barley. Add the kale and cook until just wilted. Add lemon juice, season to taste, and serve drizzled with extra virgin olive oil.

CORNED BEEF WITH BUFFALO CURD, NASHI PEAR AND BRESAOLA

Corned beef is a staple in any young Irish person's diet. This dish is an example of restraint and letting great ingredients speak for themselves. One of my favourites.

SERVES 6

INGREDIENTS

1kg silverside
1 onion, roughly chopped
1 carrot, roughly chopped
1 celery stalk, roughly chopped
1 garlic bulb, smashed
2 bay leaves
1 bunch thyme
1 bunch rosemary
1 cinnamon stick
2 star anise
pinch of fennel seeds
1 tsp black peppercorns
2 nashi pears
18 thin slices bresaola
fresh horseradish root
120g buffalo curd

METHOD

Place the meat, vegetables, garlic, herbs and spices into a large pot and cover with water. Cover and bring to a simmer over low heat, then cook for 6 hours, until tender.

Remove from the heat and allow to cool in the liquid. When cold, remove from the pot (reserve the liquid), and store, covered, in the fridge until needed.

When ready to serve, cut corned beef into squares 6cm x 6cm, and 2cm thick. Reheat to 60°C in the reserved cooking liquid. Cut the nashi pears into 6cm x 6cm slices. Place each square of beef between 2 pieces of nashi pear, and top with bresaola. Using a microplane, grate horseradish over the top. Serve with the buffalo curd.

QUAIL WITH CHIMICHURRI

SERVES 4

INGREDIENTS

3 sprigs thyme
3 garlic cloves, smashed
5 splashes olive oil
4 x 200g quail (do not debone, keep feet)
finely grated zest and juice of 1 lemon
1 handful mint, roughly chopped
1 handful flat-leaf parsley, roughly chopped
1 handful coriander, roughly chopped
1 tsp chopped habanero chilli, deseeded
½ tsp roasted and ground cumin seeds
150ml extra virgin olive oil
50g diced shallot
1 garlic clove, chopped, extra
lemon juice, to taste

METHOD

Combine the thyme, garlic and olive oil in a large plastic bag. Add the quail and seal tightly. Turn gently to coat, then place onto a tray in the fridge overnight to marinate.

Preheat the oven to 200°C. Take the quail from the bag and arrange on a baking tray. Roast for 15 minutes.

Remove from the oven, rest for 5 minutes, and drizzle with the combined lemon zest and juice. Combine the herbs, chilli, cumin, extra virgin olive oil, shallot and extra garlic. Stir in lemon juice to taste. Serve drizzled over the quail.

BLACK PUDDING AND APPLE BUTTER

SERVES 12

INGREDIENTS

BLACK PUDDING
50ml extra virgin olive oil
2 onions, diced
4 garlic cloves, sliced
3 chorizo sausages, diced
1 tsp allspice
1 tsp smoked paprika
1 tsp ground ginger
300g cooked pearl barley
300g rolled oats
300g diced back fat
2 egg yolks
1 litre pig's blood
200ml cream
vegetable oil, to fry

APPLE BUTTER
500g salted butter
5 Granny Smith apples (750g), cored, roughly chopped
1 cinnamon quill
20g ginger, finely chopped
200g caster sugar
seeds scraped from 2 vanilla beans
juice of 2 lemons

METHOD

To make the black pudding, preheat the oven to 90°C, and line a 30cm x 25cm x 5cm deep tin with cling wrap. Heat the oil in a saucepan and sweat the onions, garlic and chorizo over medium heat, until soft. Add the spices, barley, oats and back fat.

Whisk the yolks, blood and cream together, and add to the saucepan. Stir over low heat for about 5 minutes, until it starts to coagulate.

Pour into the prepared tray and cover with foil. Stand in a roasting pan, and add enough warm water to come halfway up the sides. Cook for about 20 minutes, or until set in the centre (it will be 60°C if testing with a thermometer). Remove from the roasting pan, cool, then refrigerate for 6 hours.

For the apple butter, melt the butter in a saucepan, and add the remaining ingredients, except the lemon juice. Cover and cook over low heat until soft. Remove the cinnamon stick. Blend until smooth, then pass through a fine sieve. Season with lemon juice.

To serve, use a hot knife to cut the black pudding into 1cm slices (keep dipping the knife into hot water to keep it hot). Heat the oil in a frying pan, and fry for about 1 minute each side, until dark brown. Serve with the apple butter.

NOTE
You can find pig's blood at your butcher or asian grocer.

OXTAIL WITH RISOTTO AND HORSERADISH CREAM

SERVES 6

INGREDIENTS
splash of olive oil
1 oxtail
300ml red wine
500ml port
2 litres chicken stock (approx)
2 onions, roughly chopped
2 carrots, roughly chopped
2 celery stalks, roughly chopped
1 cinnamon stick
2 star anise
1 bay leaf
5 peppercorns

HORSERADISH CREAM
250ml cream
15g hot English mustard
15g Dijon mustard
10g freshly grated horseradish
175ml crème fraîche
finely grated zest and juice of 1 lemon

RISOTTO
50g butter
1 onion, chopped
2 garlic cloves, smashed
300g arborio rice
100ml white wine
1.5 litres reserved oxtail stock, heated

METHOD
Preheat the oven to 100°C. Heat the oil in a large frying pan over high heat, and seal the oxtail on each side. Place tail into a roasting pan and deglaze with red wine and port. Pour in enough stock so it is three quarters covered. Add the vegetables.

Toast the cinnamon and star anise in a dry frying pan until fragrant. Add to the roasting pan, along with the bay leaf and peppercorns. Cover pan with foil, and bring to the boil. Place into the oven and cook for 6 hours.

Strain the stock and keep hot for the risotto (you will need 1.5 litres). Keep the vegetables aside. Leave the oxtail in the pan, cover and keep warm.

To make the horseradish cream, whip the cream with the mustards and horseradish, then fold in the crème fraîche, lemon zest and juice. Season to taste.

For the risotto, melt the butter in a large saucepan and sweat the onion and garlic over medium-low heat until soft but not coloured. Add the rice and cook, stirring, until glassy. Deglaze with the wine.

Add the hot stock a ladleful at a time, stirring constantly until absorbed between each addition.

Keep adding and stirring until the rice is al dente. Pull the meat from the oxtail and add to the risotto, along with the reserved vegetables. Season with salt and freshly ground black pepper, and serve with horseradish cream.

IRISH BREAKFAST

SERVES 1

INGREDIENTS
¼ chorizo sausage
25g black pudding (see p. 84)
2 thin slices prosciutto
50ml pork sauce (see Basics, p. 228)
1½ tbsp cooked pearl barley
splash of olive oil
1 duck egg
watercress, to garnish

CROUTONS
1 sourdough roll (day old is best)
olive oil

METHOD
To make the croutons, preheat the oven to 180°C. Thinly slice the roll into wafers, and arrange in a single layer on a baking tray. Brush with olive oil and season with salt and freshly ground black pepper. Bake until golden brown. Cool completely, then store in an airtight container if not using immediately.

Preheat the oven to 200°C. Slice the chorizo and black pudding diagonally into 5 pieces, and set aside. Rip prosciutto roughly into pieces. Heat the pork sauce and pearl barley in a saucepan.

Heat a heavy-based ovenproof frying pan over medium heat and add the oil. Gently fry the chorizo and black pudding. Once they start to colour on one side, turn over.

Crack the egg into the middle of the pan, and season with salt and freshly ground black pepper. Transfer the pan to the oven for 3 minutes, or until the white is cooked but the yolk is still runny.

Spoon the pearl barley and pork sauce around the egg. Arrange the ripped prosciutto and watercress around the egg. Season with salt and freshly ground black pepper, to taste, and serve with the croutons.

VENISON, PICKLED RED CABBAGE, BABY BEETS AND SMOKED MAYO

SERVES 4

INGREDIENTS

½ red cabbage, roughly chopped
pickling liquor (see p. 173)
50ml canola oil
2 x 300g venison (eye of round)
40g butter, diced
½ garlic bulb, smashed
3 sprigs thyme
2 baby beetroot, shaved on a mandolin
watercress sprigs, to serve

SMOKED MAYONNAISE

rock salt
300g desiree potatoes
handful hickory smoking chips
300g mayonnaise (see Basics, p. 233)
2 heaped tsp natural yoghurt
juice of 1 lemon
pinch of cayenne pepper
pinch of smoked paprika

METHOD

Place the cabbage into a glass or ceramic bowl and cover with pickling liquor. Let stand for 1 hour.

To make the smoked mayonnaise, preheat the oven to 200°C. Cover a baking tray with rock salt and place the potatoes on top. Bake for 1 hour, or until tender when pierced with a skewer. Cut in half and scoop out the flesh. Pass through a mouille, ricer or fine sieve and place into a small bowl.

Place the smoking chips into a saucepan with a steamer on top. Heat over high heat until the chips are smoking. Remove from the heat, add the bowl of mash to the steamer. Cover and leave to smoke for 2 minutes. Mix with the remaining ingredients and leave to cool. Refrigerate until required.

Preheat the oven to 180°C. Heat an ovenproof frying pan over high heat and add the oil. Sear the venison all over until lightly browned. Season with salt and freshly ground black pepper. Add the butter, garlic and thyme, and place into the oven for 2 minutes. Remove from the pan and rest in a warm place for 5 minutes (it will be 46°C when tested with a meat thermometer).

To serve, cut the venison into thick slices. Spoon mayonnaise onto serving plates, top with the venison, pickled cabbage, shaved baby beetroot and watercress sprigs. Drizzle with pan juices.

SLOWLY BRAISED BRISKET

SERVES 6

INGREDIENTS

splash of olive oil

1kg piece brisket

300ml red wine

500ml port

2 onions, roughly chopped

2 carrots, roughly chopped

2 celery stalks, roughly chopped

2 litres chicken stock

2 star anise

1 cinnamon stick

50g liquorice root

1 bay leaf

5 peppercorns

20g butter

6 pieces sourdough bread

pickled vegetables, to serve (see p. 173)

watercress sprigs, to serve

METHOD

Preheat the oven to 100°C. Heat the oil in a large frying pan over high heat. Season the meat with salt, and seal on each side. Transfer brisket to a roasting pan. Deglaze the frying pan with red wine and port then add the liquid to the roasting pan. Add the vegetables and stock.

Toast the star anise, cinnamon and liquorice root in a dry frying pan until fragrant. Add to the roasting pan, along with the bay leaf and peppercorns. Cover pan with foil, and bring to the boil. Place in the oven and cook for 6 hours. Remove from the oven and set aside, covered, for 40 minutes.

Use a spoon to break the brisket into serving portions. Foam the butter in a hot frying pan, add the bread and cook until golden brown on one side. Serve the brisket with the bread, pickled vegetables and watercress.

NOTE

Herbie's Spices supply liquorice root. Look in specialty food shops, or look for them online.

VENISON, PICKLED RED CABBAGE,
BABY BEETS AND SMOKED MAYO

SLOWLY BRAISED BRISKET

CONFIT LAMB BREAST, MISO EGGPLANT PUREE AND RED PEPPER JAM

SERVES 6

INGREDIENTS

CONFIT LAMB BREAST
4 garlic cloves, smashed
¼ bunch thyme
100g rock salt
1 ½kg lamb breast
3 litres vegetable oil, (approx.)
splash of olive oil
400g lamb leg
70g butter
1 sprig thyme
red pepper jam, to serve (see p. 15)

EGGPLANT PUREE
2 large eggplants
splash of olive oil
1 small onion, chopped
125g button mushrooms, chopped
50g light miso paste
40ml olive oil

FRIED EGGPLANT
splash of olive oil
50g butter
1 garlic clove, smashed
½ bunch thyme
1 eggplant, cut lengthways into six pieces

METHOD

For the confit lamb breast, combine the garlic, thyme and salt. Rub onto the lamb breast and leave to marinate for 2 hours.

Preheat the oven to 90°C. Brush the salt mixture off the lamb and place the lamb into a roasting pan. Pour the oil over the lamb (it should be completely covered), and cover the pan with foil. Place into the oven and cook for 4 hours, until tender. Set aside to room temperature in the oil.

Remove the lamb breast from the oil in one piece. Place between 2 trays to form a flat top and bottom. Place some weights on top (a couple of cans), and refrigerate for 6 hours.

To make the eggplant puree, char the eggplants on the stovetop until blackened all over. Place into a large bowl, cover with cling wrap and leave to steam. Once cooled a little, peel off the charred skin and roughly chop the flesh.

In a large frying pan, heat a splash of oil and sweat down the onion and mushrooms until lightly golden. Add the chopped eggplant and cook out the excess moisture. Add the miso paste, then place everything into a blender. With the motor running, add the oil slowly until it has all been added and the mixture is a smooth puree. Set aside until needed.

Preheat the oven to 180°C. Heat the oil in an ovenproof frying pan, and sear the lamb leg over high heat for 5 minutes, skin side down. Add 50g of butter and the thyme to the pan. Place pan into the oven for 5 minutes. Remove pan from oven and turn lamb over. Set aside to rest in the pan for 5 minutes. Cut into slices.

To cook the fried eggplant, heat the oil and butter in a large frying pan over high heat. Add the garlic, thyme and eggplant, and cook for 2 minutes each side or until golden brown. Drain and season.

To finish the confit lamb, cut into 6 serving portions. Melt the remaining butter in a large frying pan, and cook over low heat until golden, basting with butter. Remove from heat, rest for 2 minutes and then turn to warm other side. Season to taste.

To serve, reheat the eggplant puree and drizzle over serving plates. Add the confit lamb, lamb leg and eggplant. Serve with red pepper jam.

WHOLE ROAST CHICKEN WITH FAMOUS CHICKEN BREAD

After all the hours of slaving away roasting chickens, it's actually the bread in this dish that ends up being the show-stopper. It's crispy on the outside, soft in the middle and chock-full of chickeny goodness.

SERVES 6

INGREDIENTS

1 lemon
1 ¼kg chicken
80g butter, softened
1 garlic bulb, smashed
1 good-quality sourdough loaf
1 potato, sliced
1 bunch basil
1 bunch thyme
1 bunch tarragon
300ml extra virgin olive oil

METHOD

Preheat the oven to 200°C. Place the whole lemon inside the chicken. Combine the butter and half the garlic, and slide under the skin on the breast and thighs. Smooth the skin to spread the butter mixture.

Cut bread in half horizontally (set top half aside for another use). Slice the potato and arrange in a roasting pan for the bread to sit on. Put the bread onto the potato. Rip the herbs and scatter over the bread with the remaining garlic. Drizzle with half the oil, and season.

Place the chicken on top of the bread. Drizzle the remaining oil over the chicken, and season with salt and freshly ground black pepper.

Roast the chicken for 30 minutes, then reduce the oven to 140°C and cook a further 30 minutes. Remove from the oven and rest for 20 minutes.

Break up the chicken on the bone and cut the bread into slices. Squeeze the cooked lemon over the chicken and bread to serve.

NOTE

Serve this with the ginger and orange roast carrots (p. 160), or the iceberg salad (p. 153).

12-HOUR BRAISED LAMB SHOULDER WITH COLCANNON AND DIJON BUTTER

SERVES 4

INGREDIENTS
splash of olive oil
1kg lamb shoulder
1 carrot
1 celery
1 onion
1 bay leaf
3 sprigs thyme
3 sprigs rosemary
300ml white wine
2 litres chicken stock

COLCANNON
rock salt (to bake on)
5 desiree potatoes
100g butter
200ml milk
2 small spring onions, finely sliced
½ small bunch of cavolo nero, sliced
¼ bunch flat-leaf parsley, roughly chopped
splash of extra virgin olive oil

DIJON BUTTER
250g unsalted butter, softened
75g Dijon mustard
75g seeded mustard
20g rosemary, chopped
lemon juice, to taste

HERB CRUST
500g packaged dry breadcrumbs
40g mint leaves
40g marjoram leaves
40g curly parsley leaves
40g rosemary leaves
finely grated zest of 1 lemon

METHOD
Preheat the oven to 90°C. Heat the oil in a large frying pan over high heat, and seal lamb shoulder on each side until nicely browned. Place into an ovenproof dish with the vegetables, herbs and wine, and pour in enough stock so the meat is three quarters covered. Cover with a lid and cook for 12 hours. Remove from the oven and set aside, covered, while you make the colcannon.

For the colcannon, preheat the oven to 200°C. Cover a baking tray with rock salt and place the potatoes on top. Bake for 1 hour, or until tender when pierced with a skewer. Scoop out the flesh, and pass through a mouille, ricer or fine sieve. Place into a saucepan over low heat, and add the butter and milk. Stir until smooth, then mix in the spring onions, cavolo nero and parsley. Season with salt and freshly ground black pepper to taste, and dress with olive oil.

To make the Dijon butter, mix all the ingredients together.

For the herb crust, combine all the ingredients in a small food processor until finely chopped and well combined. Season to taste. Smear the Dijon butter over the lamb shoulder, then press the herb crust on top. Serve with the colcannon.

WHOLE ROAST LAMB WITH SMOKED HAY SAUCE AND ROAST DUCK FAT POTATOES

SERVES 6

INGREDIENTS

1 bunch basil

1 bunch rosemary

2 garlic bulbs, roughly chopped

200ml extra virgin olive oil

9kg baby lamb (milk fed)

5 handfuls of organic straw

ROAST DUCK FAT POTATOES

6 medium Sebago potatoes, peeled and quartered

375g duck fat

½ garlic bulb, smashed

1 bunch thyme, broken into sprigs

1 bunch rosemary, broken into sprigs

METHOD

Preheat the oven to 90°C. Rip the herbs and mix with garlic and oil. Rub all over the lamb, and season with salt and freshly ground black pepper

Soak the straw in 2 litres of water. Spread half the straw into a large roasting pan and place the lamb on it, with the legs pushed to belly. Cover with the remaining soaked straw, then cover the whole pan with foil. Bake for 12 hours. Remove from the oven, and set aside to rest for 40 minutes.

While the lamb is cooking, prepare the roast duck fat potatoes. Place potatoes into a saucepan and cover with cold water. Add a dash of salt, and bring to the boil. Cook over medium heat for about 15 minutes or until very tender (almost breaking apart). Drain well and place on wire rack. Cool in the fridge, uncovered, until dry.

While the lamb is resting, increase the oven temperature to 180°C. Place a roasting pan onto the stovetop, add the duck fat and heat until hot. Add the potatoes, and turn to coat.

Transfer to the oven, and cook for about 30 minutes, turning every 5 minutes, until crispy and golden.

Remove from the oven, add the garlic and herbs and fry on the stovetop for another minute to release the flavours. Drain well, and season with salt and freshly ground black pepper to taste.

Serve the lamb moistened with pan juices, with the potatoes on the side.

NOTE

Duck fat is available from most large supermarkets, poultry shops or specialist providores. Buy sterilised organic straw from farmers' markets or organic grocers.

MISO CHICKEN

Simple, comforting and light. While this makes a great restaurant dish, it's also the kind of thing I like to eat at home. Learning to make a great broth is a skill for life.

SERVES 2

INGREDIENTS

splash of olive oil

2 carrots, diced

2 onions, diced

2 celery stalks, diced

1 garlic bulb, chopped

2 bay leaves

2 star anise

300ml white wine

300g mild miso paste

2 litres chicken stock

1 chicken crown (see Note)

1 bunch pencil leeks

splash of lemon juice

METHOD

Heat the oil in a large deep pot over low heat and sweat the vegetables, garlic and bay leaves until soft but not coloured. Add the star anise and white wine and bring to the boil.

Whisk in the miso paste, add the stock and bring to the boil. Add the chicken and adjust the heat to gently simmer for 10 minutes.

Remove from the heat and leave the chicken to sit in the stock for 20 minutes. Remove from the pot, and carve the chicken meat off the bone. Strain the stock.

Blanch the leeks for 30 seconds. Refresh in iced water, then reheat in the stock. Season with salt, freshly ground black pepper and lemon juice, to taste. Serve the chicken and leeks in shallow bowls, with the stock ladled over.

NOTE

A chicken crown is the whole chicken with the legs removed. Keep the legs to make stock.

ROAST RIB EYE BEEF WITH YORKSHIRE PUDDING AND SMOKED KIPFLERS

SERVES 6

INGREDIENTS

3kg beef rib eye, tied
2 garlic cloves, smashed
¼ bunch thyme
¼ bunch rosemary
splash of olive oil
2 potatoes, thickly sliced

YORKSHIRE PUDDING

1 cup plain flour
1 ½ cups milk
1 cup eggs
vegetable oil

SMOKED KIPFLERS

24 kipfler potatoes, scrubbed
handful hickory smoking chips
vegetable oil, to deep-fry
3 spring onions, sliced
juice of 1 lemon

METHOD

Combine the beef, garlic, herbs and oil in a plastic bag. Seal and refrigerate overnight to marinate.

To start the Yorkshire pudding, whisk the flour, milk and eggs until smooth. Place into a jug, cover with cling wrap and refrigerate overnight.

Remove the beef from the fridge 2 hours before cooking. Preheat the oven to 160°C. Arrange the sliced potatoes in a roasting pan as a bed for the beef to sit on. Season with salt and freshly ground black pepper.

Sear the beef in a hot frying pan until golden brown all over. Place onto the potato, and roast for 1 hour 50 minutes, until it reaches 48°C on a meat thermometer. Remove from the oven and rest for 30 minutes.

Meanwhile, make the smoked kipflers. Place the potatoes into a saucepan and cover with cold water. Add salt, and bring to the boil. Cook over medium heat until tender when pierced with a skewer. Drain potatoes, and cool on a wire rack.

Place the smoking chips into a wide saucepan with a steamer on top. Heat over high heat until the chips are smoking. Remove from the heat, add the potatoes to the steamer (you'll need to do this in a couple of batches). Cover and leave to smoke for 2 minutes.

Half fill a saucepan with oil (or use a deep-fryer) and heat to 180°C. Deep-fry the potatoes for 2 minutes, or until golden brown. Drain on paper towel. Season with salt and serve with sliced spring onions and lemon juice.

To finish the Yorkshire pudding, increase the oven to 200°C. Place the oil into a heavy 12-hole medium muffin tray and place into the oven to preheat until extremely hot. Stir the batter, and quickly pour into tray. Bake for 10–12 minutes, until risen and golden (do not open the door during cooking). Serve immediately, with the roast beef and smoked kipflers.

PORK SHOULDER, BAKED TOMATOES AND BAKED RED ONIONS AND MUSHROOMS

A dinner party show-stopper and, best of all, simple. A must-do.

SERVES 4

INGREDIENTS

SHOULDER

1 ½kg pork shoulder, skin on

1 tsp pink salt

1 cinnamon stick

2 star anise

3 garlic cloves, left whole

2cm piece ginger, sliced

100g butter, chopped

1 bunch sage

4 tbsp apple butter (see p. 84)

sage salt, to season (see Basics, p. 226)

pork sauce (see Basics, p. 228), to serve

BAKED RED ONIONS

6 medium red onions, skin on

6 garlic cloves, left whole

splash of olive oil

100ml sherry vinegar

BAKED TOMATOES

300ml extra virgin olive oil

3 garlic cloves, smashed

½ bunch thyme

½ bunch rosemary

4 oxheart tomatoes (in season)

200g parmesan rinds

MUSHROOMS

splash of extra virgin olive oil

4 field mushrooms

30g butter

2 garlic cloves, smashed

4 sprigs thyme

splash of sherry vinegar

juice of 1 lemon

METHOD

Rub the skin of the pork shoulder with the salt. Place onto a tray and leave uncovered in the fridge overnight to dry.

Preheat oven to 220°C. Place two long lengths of foil on top of one another. In the middle, place the cinnamon, star anise, garlic, ginger, butter and half the sage.

Turn the shoulder over and season the bottom with salt and freshly ground black pepper. Place skin-side up onto the flavourings on the foil. Roll the sides of the foil up around the shoulder into a boat so when you cook the shoulder no juices escape. Leave the skin exposed.

Place the pork onto a rack in a roasting pan. Roast for 15 minutes, then reduce the oven temperature to 150°C and cook for 3 hours.

Take the pork from the oven and leave to rest for 30 minutes. Lift the skin from the flesh, spread meat with apple butter, and sprinkle with sage salt and remaining sage leaves. Replace the skin. Serve with the baked red onions, pork sauce, baked tomatoes and mushrooms.

BAKED RED ONIONS

Preheat the oven to 200°C. Place the onions and garlic into an ovenproof dish. Drizzle with oil, and season with salt and freshly ground black pepper. Bake for 30 minutes, then reduce the oven to 150°C and cook for a further 30 minutes, until soft.

Remove vegetables from the dish and add vinegar. Stir to dislodge the pan juices stuck to the base. Serve drizzled over vegetables.

BAKED TOMATOES

Preheat the oven to 100°C. Warm the oil with the garlic and herbs. Season with salt and freshly ground black pepper. Place the tomatoes into an ovenproof dish, add the warm oil mixture and the rinds. Cook for 3 hours.

MUSHROOMS

Preheat the oven to 200°C. Heat the oil in a flameproof roasting pan over medium-high heat. Add the mushrooms and brown slightly. Add the butter and cook until brown, then add the garlic and thyme.

Place into the oven and cook for 5 minutes. Remove from oven, add the sherry vinegar and lemon juice, and serve.

LAMB TONGUES WITH PICKLED CUCUMBER AND MINT JELLY

SERVES 6

INGREDIENTS

300mls white wine vinegar

100g sugar

1 tbsp salt

1 bay leaf

6 peppercorns

¼ bunch thyme

¼ bunch rosemary

9 lamb tongues

splash of extra virgin olive oil

1 cucumber, sliced lengthways

pickling liquor (see p. 173)

1 baby cos lettuce

180ml natural yoghurt

BRINE

150g salt

100g sugar

400ml red wine vinegar

2 bay leaves

1 tbsp black peppercorns

1 bunch thyme

1 garlic clove, halved

4 star anise

4 cloves

MINT JELLY

500ml sugar syrup (see Basics, p. 233)

½ bunch mint, leaves picked, stalks reserved

2½ sheets titanium gelatine

juice of 2 lemons

METHOD

For the brine, combine all the ingredients in a large pot with 1 litre of water. Bring to the boil, then cool.

Place the tongues into a large deep glass or ceramic bowl, and pour the brine over. Place into the fridge for 48 hours.

To make the mint jelly, place the syrup into a saucepan and heat until hot. Add the mint stalks. Remove from the heat and leave to infuse and cool.

Soak the gelatine leaves in cold water for 5 minutes, to soften. Squeeze out excess liquid. Add the gelatine to the syrup and stir until dissolved.

Strain the syrup and place into a blender with half of the mint leaves. Blend until the mixture turns green. Strain again, then stir in the lemon juice and season with a pinch of salt.

Pour into a 1 litre plastic container and refrigerate until set.

To cook the tongues, combine the vinegar, sugar, salt, bay leaf, peppercorns and herbs in a large pot with 1 litre of water. Drain the tongues and add to the pan. Bring to the boil. Reduce the heat to low and simmer for 40 minutes, until tender. Leave to cool in the liquid.

Preheat a chargrill to hot. Lightly oil the cucumber slices, and char for about 20 seconds. Transfer to pickling liquor and soak for 10 minutes.

Drain the tongues and peel off the skin. Cut in half horizontally and brush the cut side lightly with oil. Cook tongue oiled side down on the chargrill to sear lines, then turn 90° to sear a criss-cross pattern. Serve the tongue with cucumber, mint jelly and the lettuce dressed with yogurt. Garnish with reserved mint leaves.

ROAST PIG WITH BITTER GREENS, APPLE MATCHSTICKS AND HAM HOCK PARSNIPS

The essence of my cooking philosophy on a plate. From nose to tail, it showcases the beauty of the whole animal and will forever be a signature dish at the Four in Hand.

SERVES 10-12

INGREDIENTS

splash of olive oil

1 whole suckling pig (10kg) (see Note)

100g butter

2 garlic cloves, smashed

¼ bunch sage, leaves picked

1 Granny Smith apple

juice of 1 lemon

bitter greens, to serve

extra virgin olive oil, to dress

ham hock parsnips, to serve (see p. 161)

pork scratchings, to serve (see p. 22)

pork sauce, to serve (see Basics, p. 228)

METHOD

Preheat the oven to 200°C. Heat the oil in a large frying pan over high heat and, working in batches, cook the pork skin-side down until the skin is crisp and golden. Place into a large roasting pan, and roast for 5 minutes.

Remove from the oven, add the butter, garlic and sage and use to baste the meat. Probe each piece of meat and make sure the inside temperature is 55°C. Allow the meat to rest for 10 minutes.

Cut the apple into julienne, and toss with the lemon juice. Dress the bitter greens with extra virgin olive oil. Cut the meat into 1 cm thick slices, and arrange onto serving plates. Add the ham hock parsnips, apple matchsticks, dressed greens and small pieces of pork scratchings. Serve with pork sauce.

NOTE

Ask your butcher to break the pig into sub-primals (belly, rack, loin, leg, shoulder and neck) and use whichever part of the pig you want to, or all of it.

FISH

When cooking fish, you need to be gentle, considerate, coax it into being the best it can be. Because if you mistreat it, you're dead in the water. You have a very small window with fish, but if you get it right, it shows even greater skill than cooking meat. As a rule, I try to use sustainably sourced and locally caught fish.

Different fish require different cooking techniques, much like meat. For example, leatherjacket is great in stew, as it can take heavy cooking and big flavours. The tuna bresaola dish (p. 139), however, is cooked in a cold method with soy sauce – two different methods, two very different fish.

LIME CURED KINGFISH, CELERY AND FENNEL SNOW

SERVES 6

INGREDIENTS

500g rock salt

20g coriander seeds, toasted

250g white sugar

finely grated zest of 4 limes

finely grated zest of 2 lemons

1 side kingfish, skin off, deboned

2 celery stalks

30ml vierge dressing (see Basics, p. 227)

fennel salt (see Basics, p. 226), to taste

shaved radish, to serve

celery leaves from the inner part of the celery

FENNEL SNOW

500g fennel bulbs, roughly chopped

200ml apple juice

100ml buttermilk

5 large English spinach leaves

15g fresh ginger, peeled and chopped

75ml lemon juice

6 mint leaves

METHOD

To make the fennel snow, place all the ingredients into a blender and blend until smooth. Pass through a fine strainer, and season with salt and freshly ground black pepper. Pour into a chilled metal tray and freeze for about 8 hours (or overnight), or until solid.

Combine half the rock salt with the coriander seeds in a blender. Blend to make a fine salt. Mix with the remaining salt, and the sugar and zest.

Layer three long pieces of cling wrap on top of each other. Put half of the salt mixture into the centre of the cling wrap. Lay the fish on top, then cover with the remaining salt mixture. Tightly roll the fish and wrap with the cling wrap. Refrigerate for 3 hours.

Unroll the fish and wipe off the excess salt mixture, but don't wash under water. Cut into logs about 12cm long. Peel the celery and finely slice on an angle.

Dress the fish, celery and radishes with vierge dressing and fennel salt. Remove fennel snow from the freezer and scrape with a fork to form crystals. Spoon on top of the celery, top with radishes and celery leaves and serve immediately.

NOTE

Unused fennel snow will keep in the freezer for up to 2 weeks.

CURED TROUT

SERVES 10

INGREDIENTS

500g rock salt
250g caster sugar
10g ground black pepper
20g coriander seeds, roasted
finely grated zest of 6 lemons
finely grated zest of 6 limes
1 side ocean trout (about 1.5kg), skin off, deboned

METHOD

Using a mortar and pestle, crush the salt, sugar, pepper, coriander seeds and zest until well combined.

Line a tray with cling wrap, and spread out half the salt mixture in an area the size of the trout, about 2mm thick. Lay the trout onto the salt mixture and cover with the remaining salt mixture. Cover tightly with cling wrap.

Refrigerate for 6 hours. Brush off the salt mixture, and cut the trout into slices.

NOTE

If you like, serve this with shaved raw fennel and vierge dressing (see Basics, p. 227), or avocado puree (p. 12) and pickled vegetables (p. 173).

PICKLED MUSSELS WITH HOCK BOUILLON

SERVES 4

INGREDIENTS

1kg jumbo mussels, scrubbed and de-bearded
pickling liquor (see p. 173)
200g cannellini beans, soaked overnight in cold water
1 litre ham hock stock (see Basics, p. 232)
150ml white wine
meat from 1 ham hock, chopped (see Basics, p. 232)
splash of extra virgin olive oil
picked kale, to garnish

METHOD

Arrange the mussels in a steamer and cook over boiling water until they open. Remove from the shells, place into a glass or ceramic dish, and cover with pickling liquor. Refrigerate for 6 hours.

Meanwhile, drain the cannellini beans and place into a large saucepan. Cover with fresh cold water. Bring to a simmer, and cook for about 1 hour, until just tender but not soft. Drain.

Divide the mussels among serving bowls. Combine the stock and wine in a saucepan and bring to the boil. Remove from heat. Add the beans and hock meat. Ladle over the mussels, drizzle with extra virgin olive oil, and serve garnished with picked kale leaves.

SEARED BONITO, GINGER BEER JELLY, VANILLA CUCUMBER RIBBONS, WASABI LEAVES

SERVES 2

INGREDIENTS
300ml ginger beer
50g ginger, sliced
1 kaffir lime leaf
1 leaf titanium gelatine
Finely grated zest and juice of 1 lime
olive oil
1 bonito fillet (about 280g)
1 cucumber, shaved into ribbons
¼ vanilla pod, seeds scraped
vierge dressing (see Basics, p. 227), to taste
wasabi leaves, to serve

METHOD
Combine half the ginger beer, the ginger and lime leaf in a saucepan. Bring to the boil, then remove from the heat. Soak the gelatine in a bowl of cold water for 5 minutes, or until soft. Squeeze out excess water, then add to the warm mixture. Stir to dissolve.

Add the remaining ginger beer and lime zest to the pan. Add lime juice to taste, and season with salt and freshly ground black pepper. Strain through a fine strainer. Pour into a shallow container, and refrigerate for 1 hour or until set.

Lightly oil the fish, and season with salt. Place onto a hot grill and sear all the way round. Cut into 1.5cm slices.

To serve, scoop jelly onto plates. Arrange the sliced fish on top of the jelly. Toss the cucumber ribbons with vanilla seeds and vierge dressing. Season to taste and add to plate. Garnish with wasabi leaves.

PICKLED MUSSELS WITH HOCK BOUILLON

SEARED BONITO, GINGER BEER JELLY,
VANILLA CUCUMBER RIBBONS,
WASABI LEAVES

STEAMED BABY BARRAMUNDI WITH BEETROOT AND SMOKED EEL SAUCE, EEL BEIGNETS AND SHAVED BEETS

SERVES 4

INGREDIENTS

1 smoked eel
splash of olive oil
1 carrot, chopped
1 onion, chopped
2 celery, chopped
3 garlic cloves, chopped
100ml white wine
1½ large beetroot, washed and sliced
300ml fish stock
200ml veal stock
vegetable oil, to deep-fry
4 baby barramundi fillet (250g each)
splash of extra virgin olive oil
2 baby golden beetroot, finely shaved
small beetroot leaves, to garnish

TEMPURA BATTER

150g cornflour
150g rice flour
150g plain flour
2 egg yolks
soda water

METHOD

Cut four 25g pieces from the eel and reserve the bones (freeze left-over eel to use another time). Heat the olive oil in a pot. Add the eel bones and cook over medium-high heat until caramelised. Add the carrot, onion, celery and garlic. Cook, stirring, for 3 minutes or until lightly coloured. Deglaze with the wine.

Add two thirds of the beetroot and all the stock. Bring to a simmer and cook uncovered for 1 hour. Strain. Add the remaining beetroot and stand for 10 minutes, to infuse the colour. Strain.

Meanwhile, to make the tempura batter, sift the flours into a bowl. Add the egg yolks and enough soda water to make a batter the consistency of milk. Gently mix together — it won't be smooth. Set aside to rest for 1 hour.

To make the eel beignets, half fill a large pot with oil (or use a deep-fryer) and heat to 160°C. Dip the eel into the batter, and deep-fry for about 1 minute, until crisp. Drain on paper towels and season with salt.

Meanwhile, steam the barramundi fillets over boiling water for 4 minutes. Drizzle with extra virgin olive oil, and season with salt.

Reheat the beetroot sauce, and spoon into shallow dishes. Top with the barramundi fillets, an eel beignet and shaved golden beetroot. Garnish with beetroot leaves.

WHOLE SMOKED SAND WHITING WITH LEMON CAPER BUTTER

SERVES 4

INGREDIENTS

200g butter, softened

100g capers, finely chopped

100g cornichons, finely chopped

Finely grated zest and juice of 1 lemon

20g Dijon mustard

¼ bunch flat-leaf parsley, leaves chopped

2 x 200g whole sand whiting

hickory woodchips for smoking

splash of olive oil

METHOD

Combine the butter, capers, cornichons, lemon zest and juice, mustard and parsley. Season with salt and freshly ground pepper. Shape into a block and enclose in cling wrap. Chill until firm, then dice.

Hang the fish by the tail over a smoking pan filled with hickory woodchips (about 1 metre above it, so it is not hot enough to cook the fish) and smoke for 5 minutes.

Heat a chargrill to high heat. Brush the fish with oil and cook on the chargrill for 4–5 minutes each side.

Serve topped with lemon caper butter.

MY FISH FINGERS (WITH TARTARE SAUCE AND MUSHY PEAS)

SERVES 6

INGREDIENTS

1kg ling fillet (or your choice of firm white fish)
Finely grated zest of 1 lemon
100g plain flour
3 eggs
150ml milk
300g dry packaged breadcrumbs
vegetable oil, to deep-fry
lemon wedges, to serve

TARTARE SAUCE

250g mayonnaise (see Basics, p. 233)
50g salted baby capers, rinsed, drained
    and finely chopped
50g cornichons, finely chopped
¼ bunch flat-leaf parsley, leaves roughly chopped
finely grated zest and juice of 1 lemon

MUSHY PEAS

500g frozen peas, thawed
50g butter
½ onion, finely sliced
1 garlic clove, chopped
500ml chicken or vegetable stock
2 English spinach leaves
100g butter, softened, chopped
splash of sherry vinegar

METHOD

To make the tartare sauce, combine the mayonnaise with the capers, cornichons and parsley. Add lemon zest and juice, to taste, and season with salt and freshly ground black pepper.

To make the mushy peas, place half the peas into a blender and pulse until roughly chopped; set aside.

Melt the butter in a saucepan, add the onion and garlic and sweat over medium heat until soft but not coloured. Add the stock and bring to the boil, then add the remaining peas and cook for a few minutes without boiling so the peas heat through but retain their colour. Strain and reserve stock.

Blend the cooked peas with a splash of the stock and the spinach leaves. Add the soft butter and blend again. Mix the roughly chopped peas with the pea puree in a saucepan, and heat over low heat. Season with sherry vinegar, salt and freshly ground black pepper.

For the fish fingers, cut the fish into finger-sized batons, and sprinkle with lemon zest to lightly marinate.

Set out three bowls. Put the flour seasoned with salt and freshly ground black pepper into one, whisk the eggs and milk in the second, and put the breadcrumbs into the third. Coat the fish in the flour and shake off excess. Dip into the egg mixture then toss in the breadcrumbs, shaking off excess. Repeat the egg and crumb steps to make double-coated fish fingers.

Half fill a large pot with oil (or use a deep-fryer) and heat to 180°C. Deep-fry the fish fingers in batches until golden brown — they should be just cooked on the inside to avoid becoming dry. Drain on paper towels, and serve immediately, seasoned with salt, with the tartare sauce, mushy peas and lemon wedges.

NOTE

Tartare sauce will keep in the fridge for 1 week.

POACHED FISH AND CITRUS STEW

SERVES 4

INGREDIENTS

2 pinches saffron threads

2 large potatoes, cut into 1cm cubes

finely grated zest of 1 orange

1 leatherjacket, cut in two

1 silver dory fillet, cut in two

60ml cream

25ml lemon juice

4 pencil leeks, steamed

½ bunch broccolini, steamed

4 pencil fennel, steamed

STOCK

1¼kg fish bones (whole frames)

2 carrots, roughly chopped

3 celery stalks, roughly chopped

1 head fennel, roughly chopped (reserve fronds)

2 onions, roughly chopped

5 garlic cloves

600ml orange juice

500g canned tomatoes

½ bunch thyme

2 bay leaves

5 star anise, toasted

1 tsp fennel seeds, toasted

1 tsp coriander seeds, toasted

ROUILLE

1 garlic bulb

olive oil, to drizzle

3 sprigs thyme

10 saffron threads

3 hardboiled egg yolks

3 egg yolks

3 anchovies

juice of 1 lemon

500ml olive oil

smoked paprika, to taste

METHOD

To make the rouille, preheat the oven to 140°C. Cut the garlic bulb in half and place onto a square of foil. Drizzle with a little oil and place the thyme sprigs on top. Enclose in the foil, and roast for about 1½ hours, or until soft. Cool before using.

Place the saffron into 1 tablespoon of warm water for a few minutes to bleed the colour. Squeeze half the garlic from the skin into a blender (save the rest for another use), and add the cooked and raw egg yolks, anchovies and lemon juice. Blitz until smooth.

With the motor running, gradually add the oil in a thin stream. Season with paprika and salt and freshly ground black pepper.

To make the stock, combine all the ingredients in a large pot, and add enough water to cover. Bring to the boil, then reduce the heat and simmer for 1 hour, skimming any impurities from the top. Strain through a fine sieve.

To poach the fish, drop saffron into a saucepan of cold water and allow colour to bleed. Season with salt and freshly ground black pepper. Add the potatoes and bring to the boil. As soon as the water boils, cover the pan with a lid and remove from the heat. Leave the potatoes to cool in the saffron water. When cold, the potatoes should be just cooked and have taken on the colour from the saffron.

Combine the strained stock in a saucepan with the orange zest, and bring to a simmer. Add the leatherjacket and simmer for 3 minutes. Add the dory and potatoes and simmer for a further 2 minutes. Gently lift out the fish and potatoes and place into a serving dish. Put the stock back on the heat and add the cream and lemon juice. Season with salt to taste. Pour over the fish and garnish with the steamed vegetables and fennel fronds.

WHOLE STEAMED FLOUNDER IN FENNEL

A simple, steamed fish dish, with a big wow factor. When you peel back the fennel, you unleash a plume of scented steam and unveil the whole fish in all its glory.

SERVES 2

INGREDIENTS

1 large potato, peeled and cut into 3cm slices

200ml white wine

90ml pernod

ripped fennel tops (enough to cover fish top and bottom)

1 large whole flounder (800g), scaled

1 lemon, sliced

3 bay leaves

6 sprigs lemon thyme

1 garlic bulb, sliced

METHOD

Preheat the oven to 180°C. Arrange the potato slices over the base of a roasting pan (large enough to hold the fish). The potatoes act as a base to prevent the fish from overcooking.

Combine the wine and pernod with 1 litre of water in a saucepan. Season with salt and bring to the boil. Pour the water mixture into the pan, then sprinkle with half the fennel tops.

Lay the fish onto the potatoes, and top with the lemon slices. Season with salt and freshly ground black pepper, then add the bay leaves, thyme, garlic and remaining fennel tops. Cover the pan tightly with foil and bake for 10 minutes, or until flesh flakes easily when tested with the back of a spoon.

Stand for 2 minutes, then serve the fish with the strained pan juices as a sauce.

NOTE

This is a great way to use up left-over fennel tops.

CONFIT TROUT WITH APPLE AND SORREL JUICE

SERVES 4

INGREDIENTS

250ml apple juice

1 bunch sorrel

lemon juice, to taste

1 litre olive oil

1 garlic clove, smashed

1 sprig thyme

400g ocean trout fillet, cut into 4 pieces

seaweed salt (see Basics, p. 226)

olive oil, extra, to serve

baby sorrel leaves, to garnish

METHOD

Blend the apple juice, sorrel and lemon juice together. Strain, and place into the fridge to chill.

Place the olive oil, garlic and thyme into a wide, deep frying pan, and heat to 60°C. Take off the heat, add the trout pieces and return to very low heat. Slowly heat until the inside of the fish is 40°C when tested with a thermometer. Remove from oil and drain on paper towel.

Coat the top of the trout with seaweed salt. Serve with the apple and sorrel juice, and drizzle with the extra olive oil. Garnish with baby sorrel leaves to serve.

TUNA 'BRESAOLA' WITH BUTTERMILK CURD AND CELERY

SERVES 4

INGREDIENTS

250g piece grade-A sashimi tuna

4 celery stalks, peeled and cut into 4cm lengths

extra virgin olive oil, to finish

fennel fronds, to garnish

SOY MARINADE

250ml soy sauce

60ml sugar syrup (see Basics, p. 233)

50ml white wine vinegar

10g fresh ginger, grated

1 star anise

1 cinnamon stick

1 tsp juniper berries

1 tsp fennel seeds

BUTTERMILK CURD

600ml carton buttermilk

200g natural yoghurt

100ml extra virgin olive oil

finely grated zest and juice of 1 lemon

pinch of salt

METHOD

For the soy marinade, combine all the ingredients in a saucepan and bring to the boil. Let cool before using.

Pour the marinade into a shallow glass or ceramic dish. Add the tuna, making sure it is completely submerged. Cover and refrigerate for 48 hours.

Meanwhile, to make the buttermilk curd, place the buttermilk carton into a saucepan. Add enough water to come right up to the top. Slowly bring to a simmer over low heat. Simmer for 30 minutes, remove from pan and allow to cool in carton.

When cold, strain the resulting curd through a fine sieve. Whisk the yoghurt, oil, lemon zest and juice, and salt into the curd.

To serve, remove the tuna from the marinade, and cut into thin slices. Fill a piping bag with the buttermilk curd, and use to fill the celery stalks. Cover with tuna slices. Arrange on a plate with a few extra dots of curd, and finish with extra virgin olive oil and fennel fronds.

NOTE

Left-over curd will keep in the fridge for up to 1 week.

CONFIT TROUT WITH APPLE AND SORREL JUICE

WHOLE ROAST MULLOWAY, VANILLA CLAMS AND FENNEL

SERVES 6

INGREDIENTS

splash of extra virgin olive oil

3 large fennel, quartered

3 onions, peeled and halved

½ garlic bulb, peeled and finely sliced

2 bay leaves

½ bunch thyme

200ml white wine

1 litre fish stock

200ml cream

½ vanilla bean, seeds scraped

2kg mulloway (whole), cleaned

knob of soft butter

1kg diamond shell clams

wide strips of rind cut from 1 lemon

lemon salt (see Basics, p. 226)

METHOD

Preheat the oven to 200°C. Heat the oil in a flameproof roasting pan. Add the fennel, onion and garlic, and sweat over medium heat until soft but not coloured. Add the bay leaves and thyme.

Deglaze with the white wine. Add the stock and bring to the boil. Add the cream and bring to the boil once more, season with salt and freshly ground black pepper, and add the vanilla seeds.

Score the skin of the fish and rub with butter. Place the fish and clams on top of the fennel and onions. Season with lemon rind and lemon salt. Roast for 15 minutes.

ROAST MARRON

SERVES 4

INGREDIENTS

splash of extra virgin olive oil
2 marron (40g each)
20g butter
3 sprigs thyme
½ bulb garlic, smashed
4 baby fennel, blanched
4 baby leeks, blanched
1 litre prawn bisque (see p. 36)
5 desiree potatoes, diced and blanched
2 sprigs tarragon
½ bunch basil, leaves picked
2 spring onions, finely sliced
finely grated zest and juice of 1 lemon

METHOD

Preheat the oven to 210°C. Heat the oil in a small flameproof roasting pan over high heat. Cook the marron for 1 minute each side.

Add the butter, thyme and garlic. Transfer pan to the oven and cook for 2 minutes. Turn marron and cook a further 2 minutes. Remove from the oven and set aside to rest for 5 minutes. Cut the marron in half and remove the intestinal tract. Crack the claws.

Meanwhile, heat the fennel and leeks in the bisque. Add the potatoes, marron, tarragon, basil and spring onions. Season with salt and freshly ground black pepper, to taste, and add the lemon zest and juice.

NOTE

You can use lobster instead of marron if you like.

SPANISH MACKEREL WITH SOFT AND CRISP ARTICHOKES AND PRUNES

SERVES 4

INGREDIENTS

500g rock salt
500g Jerusalem artichokes
½ 375g can prunes, pitted
100ml Pedro Ximénez sherry
100ml extra virgin olive oil
juice of 1 lemon
vegetable oil, to deep-fry
splash of olive oil
720g roast Spanish mackerel, cut into 4 pieces
20g butter
1 garlic clove, crushed
1 sprig thyme
splash extra virgin olive oil
lemon juice, to taste

METHOD

Preheat the oven to 150°C. Cover a baking tray with rock salt and place the artichokes on top. Bake for 45 minutes or until tender when pierced with a skewer. Cool, then cut in half and scrape out the flesh, keeping the skins in large pieces. Increase the oven temperature to 200°C.

Heat the prunes, prune liquid and sherry in a saucepan. Stir in the extra virgin olive oil and half the lemon juice. Season with salt and freshly ground black pepper.

Half fill a saucepan with vegetable oil and heat to 140°C. Deep-fry the artichoke skins until golden. Drain on paper towels, and season with salt.

Heat a splash of olive oil in an ovenproof frying pan over high heat. Add the fish and cook until golden on each side. Place the pan in the oven and cook for two minutes on each side. Remove the pan from the oven and place over medium heat. Working quickly, add the butter, garlic, thyme and remaining lemon juice. Baste twice, and remove fish from pan.

Reheat the soft artichokes and season with salt, freshly ground black pepper, extra virgin olive oil and lemon juice. Slice the fish, and serve with the soft and crisp artichokes, and the drained prunes.

VEGIES AND SIDES

Vegetables and side dishes are the part of the menu that I've only really come to love in the past few years. I used to think 'vegetables' was a dirty word, but as I've grown older, healthier and wiser, vegetables now play a huge role in my life.

Vegetable dishes can require as much skill as cooking the most delicate fish. Roasted celeriac (p. 170) is as difficult to pull off as a piece of braised brisket (p. 91).

Vegetables make a meal, even sometimes the whole meal.

MIXED GRAIN SALAD

If you are ever going to make a salad in your life, this is the one. It's textural and substantial, light and nourishing.

SERVES 12

INGREDIENTS

200g red quinoa
200g white quinoa
200g pearl barley
splash of olive oil
½ onion, cut into large pieces
½ carrot, cut into large pieces
1 celery stalk, cut into large pieces
¼ bunch thyme
1 bay leaf
200g Puy lentils
200g unsalted butter
1 garlic clove, crushed
1 sprig thyme
50g pumpkin seeds
50g sunflower seeds
50g chopped almonds, skin on
½ bunch mint, leaves roughly chopped
½ bunch flat-leaf parsley, leaves roughly chopped
100ml sherry dressing (see Basics, p. 227)
100ml vierge dressing (see Basics, p. 227)

METHOD

Place red quinoa and white quinoa into separate large saucepans and cover with water about 1cm above the surface of the grains. Cover and bring to the boil, then reduce the heat and simmer, covered, for 10 minutes or until the grains are tender but still have a little bite (the red quinoa will take slightly longer to cook). Drain and cool completely.

Meanwhile, preheat the oven to 180°C. Spread the pearl barley onto a baking tray and put in the oven for about 10 minutes, until golden brown. This gives a nice nutty flavour. Transfer the toasted barley to a pot and cover with water. Bring to the boil, reduce the heat and simmer for 10–12 minutes, or until just soft. Drain and cool completely.

To prepare the lentils, heat the oil in a large saucepan and sweat the onion, carrot and celery over medium-high heat for about 5 minutes. Add the thyme and bay leaf. Once the vegetables have started to break down slightly, add the lentils and cover with water. Bring to the boil then reduce the heat and simmer for 10–12 minutes, or until just tender. Strain and pick out the vegetables and herbs.

Heat the butter in a frying pan until foaming, and add the garlic and thyme. Add the seeds and nuts, and cook over medium heat for 5 minutes, until toasted. Drain on paper towels and cool.

Mix all the grains and toasted nuts with the mint and parsley. Add the dressings, season with pink salt and pepper, and toss to combine.

ICEBERG WITH SALAD CREAM AND PARMESAN

SERVES 8

INGREDIENTS
1 iceberg lettuce
4 radishes
25g parmesan

CROUTONS
1 sourdough roll (day-old is best)
olive oil

SALAD CREAM
25ml evaporated milk
2 tsp white wine vinegar (optional, see Note)
250ml mayonnaise (see Basics, p. 233)
sugar and salt, to taste

METHOD
To make the croutons, preheat the oven to 180°C. Thinly slice the roll into wafers, and arrange in a single layer on a baking tray. Brush with olive oil and season with salt and freshly ground black pepper. Bake until golden brown. Cool completely, then store in an airtight container if not using immediately.

To make the salad cream, add enough evaporated milk and vinegar (if using) to the mayonnaise to make a thick pouring consistency. Season with sugar and salt, to taste.

Rip the iceberg lettuce into 8 rough portions. Using a mandolin, finely shave the radish. Arrange on serving plates. Open each layer of lettuce and add a good dollop of salad cream, add the croutons, grate parmesan over the salad, and serve.

NOTE
Depending on the sharpness of the mayonnaise you use, vinegar may not be necessary. Taste it to check before adding.

GNOCCHI

SERVES 8

INGREDIENTS

1kg rock salt (to bake on)
1kg desiree potatoes
¼ bunch thyme
¼ bunch sage
¼ bunch mint
110g plain flour
pinch of salt
2 egg yolks
splash of olive oil
50g unsalted butter
2 garlic cloves, crushed
4 sprigs thyme

METHOD

Preheat the oven to 200°C. Cover a baking tray with rock salt and place the potatoes on top. Bake for 1 hour, or until tender when pierced with a skewer.

Pick leaves from the herbs, and roughly chop. Combine the herbs, flour and salt.

Cut the potatoes in half and scoop out the insides. Pass through a ricer onto a lightly floured work surface. Add the egg yolks and combine quickly so the yolks don't cook before they are incorporated.

Add the flour mixture in three batches, mixing gently until just combined. Don't overwork the dough, or the gnocchi will be tough.

Divide the dough into 6 portions, and roll into logs about 2cm thick. Using a floured palette knife, cut into pieces about 3cm long.

Bring a large pot of salted water to the boil then reduce to a simmer. Drop one third of the gnocchi into the water. Once gnocchi has risen to the surface, give it 30 seconds then use a slotted spoon to scoop it out, and transfer it to a bowl of iced water to stop the cooking. Drain, then drizzle with olive oil and store in fridge until needed. Repeat with remaining gnocchi in 2 more batches.

To reheat, preheat the oven to 200°C. Heat a large ovenproof frying pan over high heat and add a splash of oil. Add half the gnocchi, and gently colour on both sides. Transfer pan to the oven for about 4 minutes or until golden. Set gnocchi aside. Repeat with remaining gnocchi. Add all the gnocchi to the pan with the butter, garlic and thyme. Toss over medium heat to baste with the butter. Season with salt and freshly ground black pepper, and serve immediately.

NOTE

Choose evenly sized potatoes so they cook at the same time. To freeze gnocchi, place in a single layer onto a tray and cover with plastic wrap. Once firm, place into an airtight container in layers, with sheets of plastic wrap or baking paper between. No need to thaw, just cook as directed.

SWEDE GRATIN

The vegetable of my childhood, which I have fallen in love with all over again as an adult. This dish is a meal in itself.

SERVES 6–8

INGREDIENTS

1kg swede
1 onion
3 garlic cloves
40g unsalted butter, chopped
100ml white wine
800ml cream
50g cheddar cheese, grated

METHOD

Preheat the oven to 150°C. Finely slice the swede, onion and garlic (a mandolin is best for this). Melt the butter in a large saucepan, and add the onion and garlic. Sweat over medium-low heat until soft but not coloured.

Add the wine and bring to the boil. Add the cream, season with salt and freshly ground black pepper. Simmer for 3 minutes.

Layer the swede and the onion mixture into a medium ovenproof frying pan or dish to make four layers in total. Make sure you finish with a layer of cream. Sprinkle with the cheese.

Place the pan onto a baking tray to catch any spills during cooking. Cover with foil and bake for 1 hour. Remove the foil and bake for a further 30 minutes, until the top is golden brown. Allow to sit for 30 minutes before serving.

FRESH FENNEL, PEA, FETA AND YOGHURT SALAD

SERVES 4

INGREDIENTS
2 fennel bulbs
50g fresh peas, blanched and refreshed
½ bunch mint, leaves picked
100g organic natural yoghurt
smoked paprika, to taste
extra virgin olive oil, to taste
100g Danish feta
vierge dressing (see Basics, p. 227), to serve

METHOD
Finely shave the fennel (a mandolin is best for this). Combine the peas, mint and yoghurt with the shaved fennel, and season with smoked paprika, salt and freshly ground black pepper, to taste.

Drizzle with extra virgin olive oil, and crumble the feta over the top. Serve with vierge dressing.

LETTUCE AND LOVAGE

SERVES 4

INGREDIENTS
200ml chicken stock
50ml white wine
20g unsalted butter
2 baby cos lettuce
2 bunches lovage, leaves picked
juice of ½ lemon

METHOD
Combine the stock and wine in a large, deep frying pan, and bring to the boil. Add the butter to the pan, and whisk to combine. Simmer for 2 minutes, and season with salt and freshly ground black pepper, to taste.

Remove the pan from the heat. Rip the lettuce leaves, and roughly chop the lovage. Add to the pan along with the lemon juice, and allow to wilt slightly. Serve immediately.

NOTE
Lovage is a leafy herb with a flavour reminiscent of celery. Look for it at farmers' markets, or ask your greengrocer to source some for you. It can easily be grown in a home vegetable garden.

GINGER AND ORANGE ROAST CARROTS WITH CUMIN YOGHURT

SERVES 6

INGREDIENTS

4 bunches mixed heirloom baby carrots,
    scrubbed, tops trimmed
100g ginger, roughly chopped
2 star anise
¼ bunch thyme
4 garlic cloves, smashed
1 litre orange juice
30g unsalted butter

CUMIN YOGHURT

10g cumin seeds
500ml natural yoghurt
¼ bunch mint, leaves roughly chopped
paprika, to taste

METHOD

Place the carrots, ginger, star anise, half the thyme and 2 garlic cloves into a medium-large saucepan. Add the orange juice. Bring to the boil, reduce the heat slightly and cook for 5 minutes, or until just tender. Drain.

Melt the butter in a frying pan. Add the carrots with the remaining thyme and garlic, and cook for 10 minutes, turning every few minutes, until golden brown all over. Season with salt and freshly ground black pepper, to taste.

To make the cumin yoghurt, dry roast the cumin seeds until fragrant, then crush using a mortar and pestle. Combine with the yoghurt and mint, and season with paprika, salt and freshly ground black pepper.

Transfer the carrots to a serving dish, season and dress with cumin yoghurt.

NOTE

The juice from cooking the carrots can be kept, frozen, to use again.

HAM HOCK PARSNIPS

SERVES 8

INGREDIENTS

300ml ham hock stock (see Basics, p. 232)
4 parsnips, halved lengthways
10g unsalted butter
½ bunch thyme
2 bay leaves
2 garlic cloves, smashed

METHOD

Preheat the oven to 180°C. Place the stock into a deep ovenproof frying pan, and bring to the boil. Add the parsnips and cook for 5 minutes. Remove from the pan and set aside.

Add the butter, thyme, bay leaves and garlic to the stock, and cook until reduced by half. Add the parsnips and turn to glaze.

Place the pan into the oven and bake for about 10 minutes, or until glazed and sticky.

GINGER AND ORANGE
ROAST CARROTS WITH
CUMIN YOGHURT

BRAISED CELERY HEARTS

SERVES 4

INGREDIENTS

splash of olive oil

2 whole celery hearts and leaves, halved lengthways

100ml white wine

10g fennel seeds, toasted and smashed

2 garlic cloves, smashed

½ bunch thyme

3 bay leaves

20g unsalted butter

300ml chicken stock

celery salt, to taste (see Basics, p. 226)

METHOD

Preheat the oven to 200°C. Heat the oil in an ovenproof frying pan. Add the celery hearts and cook over medium heat until golden. Deglaze the pan with white wine, then add the fennel seeds, garlic, herbs, butter and stock.

Transfer to the oven and cook for about 40 minutes, basting the celery every 10 minutes, until golden and sticky.

Serve seasoned with celery salt.

GRILLED BABY LEEKS WITH PARMESAN

SERVES 6

INGREDIENTS

2 bunches baby (pencil) leeks
50g Reggiano parmesan

METHOD

Remove the first layer from the leeks and wash well to remove any dirt. Leave the roots intact.

Blanch the leeks in a pan of boiling salted water for 1 minute, then plunge into a bowl of iced water to stop the cooking and preserve the colour.

Preheat a chargrill to hot. Cook the leeks for about 2 minutes, turning to cook evenly, until chargrilled.

Place the leeks onto a serving plate. Finely grate parmesan over, and season with salt and freshly ground black pepper.

2-HOUR COOKED BUTTERED LEEKS

SERVES 4

INGREDIENTS

2 large leeks
300g unsalted butter
½ bunch thyme
2 garlic cloves, smashed

METHOD

Preheat the oven to 100°C. Remove the first layer from the leeks and cut off the green tops. Cut the leeks in half lengthways, with the root intact. Wash well to remove any dirt.

Melt the butter in a flameproof roasting pan on the stovetop, and season with salt and freshly ground black pepper. Arrange the leeks in the pan and add the thyme and garlic.

Allow the leeks to fry for 30 seconds. Cover the pan with foil and place into the oven for 2 hours.

Remove and season with more salt and pepper.

CELERIAC 3 WAYS

The outer crust of slow-cooked celeriac takes on a meaty flavour. This vegetable dish stands up to any meat dish in substance and style.

SERVES 4

INGREDIENTS

ROAST CELERIAC

1 large celeriac, quartered
200g unsalted butter
3 sprigs thyme
3 sprigs rosemary
3 garlic cloves, crushed

CELERIAC PUREE

splash of vegetable oil
1 onion, chopped
2 garlic cloves, chopped
1kg celeriac, peeled and chopped
¼ bunch thyme
1 bay leaf
350ml cream
300ml milk
50g unsalted butter, chopped

CELERIAC CHIPS

½ celeriac
good splash of olive oil

METHOD

To make the roast celeriac, preheat the oven to 130°C. Clean and peel the celeriac, leaving about 1 cm of root on top. Cut into quarters.

Melt the butter in a roasting pan on the stovetop. Place the celeriac into the pan with the herbs and garlic. Keep turning the celeriac in the foaming butter until lightly golden all over. Season with salt and freshly ground black pepper. Transfer to the oven and cook for 3 hours, turning every 20 minutes, to maintain an even colour. Remove from pan and drain on paper towel. Serve immediately, or reheat slowly when needed.

For the celeriac puree, heat the oil in a large saucepan. Sweat the onions and garlic over medium-low heat until they start to break down. Add the celeriac to the pan with the herbs, cream and milk.

Bring to the boil, then reduce the heat slightly and simmer, uncovered, until the celeriac is completely soft. Cool slightly, remove the herbs, then blend with the butter until smooth. Season to taste. Serve immediately, or reheat gently to serve.

For the celeriac chips, preheat the oven to 140°C. Clean and peel the celeriac, and cut in half again. Finely slice on a mandolin, as thin as you can. Toss with olive oil, and season with salt and freshly ground black pepper.

Line 2 large baking trays with baking paper, and layer celeriac chips onto them in a single layer. Bake for about 15 minutes, or until golden and becoming crispy. Turn over halfway through cooking. Cool slightly before serving (they will become crisper on cooling).

To serve, spoon celeriac puree onto a serving plate, top with roast celeriac and celeriac chips. Drizzle with extra virgin olive oil.

PICKLED VEGETABLES

MAKES 2 MEDIUM JARS

INGREDIENTS

PICKLING LIQUOR

1 cinnamon stick

3 star anise

300ml white wine vinegar

150g white sugar

2 bay leaves

¼ bunch thyme

20g salt

VEGETABLES

1 cucumber

1 bunch baby carrots, peeled and halved

1 bunch baby turnips, thickly sliced

1 bunch radishes, thickly sliced

¼ cauliflower, broken into small florets

1 bunch spring onions, trimmed and halved

METHOD

To make the pickling liquor, place the cinnamon and star anise into a saucepan, and dry roast over medium heat for about 1 minute, or until fragrant. Add the remaining ingredients with 450ml water and bring to the boil.

Combine all the vegetables in a large non-metallic bowl. Pour the hot pickling liquor over the vegetables (it needs to cover them), and leave for 6 hours.

To store, transfer to sterilised jars and keep for up to 4 weeks.

DESSERTS

Pastry is an art in itself and there's a reason some chefs choose to specialise in all things sweet. Desserts have to be precise, often refined. Unlike meat, you can't add a little, take away a little, as you go. Desserts are the parting shot when it comes to the meal, and they're often the thing people remember most.

The desserts I like best are the ones that challenge me. I like to use less predictable ingredients (like those not necessarily associated with desserts), and a little nostalgia goes a long way, too. My bounty dish (p. 176) is a good example. Seasons also play a role, and in order to make a good dessert great, all you need to do is steal a pinch or two of spice from that season to make it feel current. Mother Nature has done all the hard work, so use what you find at hand. Quinces in winter, strawberries in summer ... using the seasons is practical – it's produce at its peak.

BOUNTY

SERVES 10

INGREDIENTS

COCONUT ICE-CREAM
200g desiccated coconut
500ml milk
2 litres cream
200g liquid glucose
24 egg yolks
200g caster sugar

COCONUT FUDGE
225g unsalted butter, chopped
680g caster sugar
375ml can evaporated milk
170g white chocolate, chopped
150g desiccated coconut, toasted

COCONUT SHARDS
1 coconut

CHOCOLATE DELICE
375g caster sugar
18 egg yolks
2 1/4 litres cream, whipped to soft peaks
1kg dark chocolate (70%), melted (still slightly warm)

CHOCOLATE CRACK
225ml orange juice
60g liquid glucose
75g unsalted butter, chopped
5g pectin
300g sugar
180g plain flour
35g cocoa powder

TO FINISH
dark cocoa powder

METHOD

To make the coconut ice-cream, preheat the oven to 160°C. Spread the coconut onto a baking tray and cook for about 5 minutes, stirring occasionally so it cooks evenly, until golden.

Combine the milk, cream and glucose in a large saucepan. Heat until almost boiling, then remove from the heat and stir in the toasted coconut. Leave to infuse for 2 hours.

Strain the coconut mixture into a clean saucepan and bring back to the boil. Whisk the egg yolks and sugar in a bowl until light and fluffy. Slowly pour the hot coconut-infused milk into the egg mixture, while whisking constantly. Return to the saucepan and stir constantly until the mixture thickens and coats the back of a spoon.

Pour into a bowl sitting on another bowl filled with ice, to stop the cooking. Stir often to release the heat, then place into the fridge until chilled. Churn in an ice-cream machine according to manufacturer's instructions. Transfer to an airtight container and freeze until firm.

For the coconut fudge, line a 30cm x 25cm x 5cm pan with greaseproof paper. Combine the butter, sugar and evaporated milk in a large saucepan over medium heat. Place a sugar thermometer into the pan, and bring the mixture to 120°C. Whisk continuously as the mixture can catch and burn easily (it will be quite thick).

Remove from the heat and add the white chocolate and coconut. Stir until the chocolate has melted, then pour into the prepared pan. Place into the fridge for at least 30 minutes, to set.

To make the coconut shards, preheat the oven to 180°C. Place the coconut into the oven for 20 minutes. Reduce oven to 90°C. Crack coconut open and use a butter knife to pop out the flesh. Shave the coconut flesh with a peeler and spread onto a baking tray. Toast in the oven until golden brown.

For the chocolate delice, place the sugar into a saucepan and add enough water to cover. Stir over low heat until sugar has dissolved, then increase the heat and bring to the boil. Place a sugar thermometer into the pan and cook until it reaches soft ball stage (118°C).

Meanwhile, whisk the egg yolks in an electric mixer until light and fluffy. With the motor running, pour the sugar syrup slowly onto the yolks. Whisk on high until cool.

Add a little of the whipped cream to the chocolate to loosen it (if you add the egg mixture first, it will set hard), then carefully fold in the egg mixture and remaining cream until just combined. Place into the fridge for 30 minutes.

To make the chocolate crack, combine the orange juice, glucose and butter in a saucepan and bring to the boil. Mix the pectin through the sugar then add to the orange juice mixture. Bring back to the boil and cook for 3 minutes.

Sift the flour and cocoa powder into a large mixing bowl. Make a well in the centre and add the hot liquid. Whisk the flour in slowly until smooth. Refrigerate for about 1 hour until the mixture is a firm but spreadable consistency.

Preheat the oven to 180°C. Divide the mixture in half and spread out as thinly as possible onto 2 sheets of greaseproof paper. Place onto large baking trays and use a non-serrated knife to score 12 rectangles into each batch, making each portion slightly larger than the parfait bars. Bake for 8 minutes. The mixture should bubble and go quite dark. Lift off tray and leave to cool. It should be crisp enough to snap along scored lines. If not, it will need a little longer in the oven.

To assemble, spread delice onto plates. Scoop about 5 small balls of coconut ice-cream on top. Dust with cocoa powder. Use a vegetable peeler to shave coconut fudge over the dessert and place some toasted coconut shards around. Break the chocolate crack into shards and add to the plate. It should look quite messy and you should be able to get some of each component in each spoonful.

NOTE

You will find pectin in a health food shop.

BOUNTY

WHITE CHOCOLATE SANDWICH

WHITE CHOCOLATE SANDWICH

If we took this off the menu at 4Fourteen, we would have to close the doors. Ice-cream sandwiches take me back to my childhood; we'd be given them after dinner on Sundays and they were always something to look forward to.

SERVES 12

INGREDIENTS

PARFAIT
185g caster sugar
15 egg yolks
350g white chocolate
900ml cream

CHOCOLATE CRACK
225ml orange juice
60g liquid glucose
75g unsalted butter, chopped
5g pectin
300g sugar
180g plain flour
35g cocoa powder

DULCE DE LECHE
2 x 390g cans condensed milk
50 ml cream

METHOD

To make the parfait, place the sugar into a saucepan and add 50ml water. Stir over low heat until sugar has dissolved, then increase the heat and bring to the boil. Place a sugar thermometer into the pan and boil until it reaches 118°C (soft ball stage).

Put the egg yolks into the bowl of an electric mixer and whisk on high until light and fluffy. Reduce the speed to low, and with the motor running gradually add the sugar syrup. Turn the speed back up to high and whisk until cool.

Break up the chocolate and place into a bowl sitting over a saucepan of simmering water (make sure the bottom of the bowl is not touching the water). Once softened, stir until melted and smooth. Add to the egg mixture and keep whisking until combined.

Whip the cream in a large bowl to form soft peaks. Fold the cream through the egg and chocolate mixture one third at a time. Line a 30cm x 25cm x 5cm pan with a few layers of cling wrap. Pour the mixture into the tray and freeze overnight.

Place a plastic chopping board into the freezer for 30 minutes. Turn the frozen mixture out onto the chilled board, and remove the cling wrap. Cut into 12 bars. Place onto a tray lined with baking paper, cover with cling wrap and return to the freezer until needed.

For the dulce de leche, place the cans of condensed milk on their sides into a large saucepan and cover completely with water. Cover the pan with a lid, and bring to the boil. Tilt the lid slightly, and cook for 4 hours, topping up with boiling water as needed (cans must be submerged at all times). Cool completely before opening the cans. Scoop into a bowl and chill. Just before serving, whisk in the cream.

To make the chocolate crack, combine the orange juice, glucose and butter in a saucepan and bring to the boil. Mix the pectin through the sugar then add to orange juice mixture. Bring back to the boil and cook for 3 minutes.

Sift the flour and cocoa powder into a large mixing bowl. Make a well in the centre and add the hot liquid. Whisk the flour in slowly until smooth. Refrigerate for about 1 hour until the mixture is a firm but spreadable consistency.

Preheat the oven to 180°C. Divide the mixture in half and spread out as thinly as possible onto 2 sheets of greaseproof paper. Place onto large baking trays and use a non-serrated knife to score 12 rectangles into each portion, slightly larger than the parfait bars. Bake for 8 minutes. The mixture

should bubble and go quite dark. Lift off tray and leave to cool. It should be crisp enough to snap along scored lines. If not, it will need a little longer in the oven.

To assemble, place 1 piece of chocolate crack onto each serving plate. Top with a bar of parfait, and pipe dulce de leche along the bar. Sandwich with another piece of chocolate crack, and pipe a dollop of the remaining dulce de leche alongside.

NOTE
You will find pectin in a health food shop.

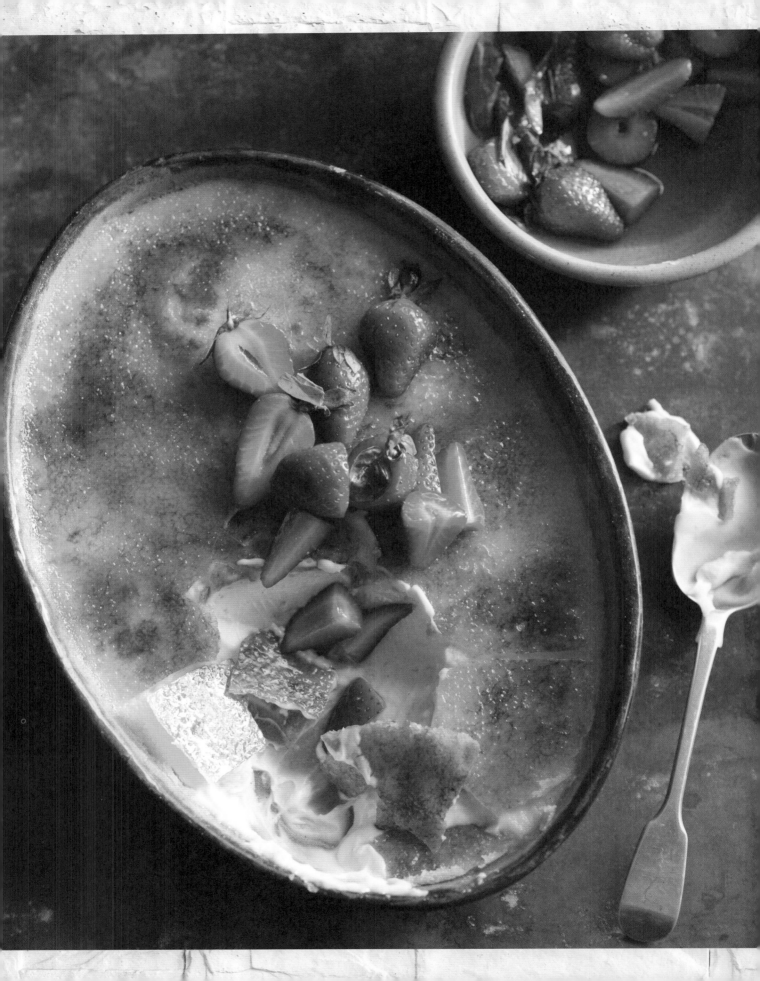

BASIL BRÛLÉE WITH MACERATED STRAWBERRIES

SERVES 8–10

INGREDIENTS

100ml milk
900ml cream
1 vanilla bean, split, seeds scraped
1 bunch basil
145g caster sugar
16 egg yolks
200g caster sugar, extra, for topping

MACERATED STRAWBERRIES

2 punnets strawberries
100g sugar
50ml raspberry vinegar
seeds scraped from 1/2 vanilla bean
lemon juice, to taste

METHOD

Preheat the oven to 95°C. Combine the milk, cream, vanilla bean and seeds in a saucepan over medium heat. Bring to the boil, then add the basil (stalks and all) and stand for 20 minutes, to infuse.

Whisk the sugar and egg yolks together until light and creamy, and pour the warm cream over, whisking constantly. Strain through a fine sieve.

Pour the mixture into a 1.5 litre shallow ovenproof dish. Stand dish in a roasting pan and pour in enough water to come halfway up the sides of the dish. Cook for 1½–2 hours, until just set (it will be 80°C in the centre if testing with a thermometer). Lift from the water bath and cool slightly, then refrigerate until chilled.

For the macerated strawberries, roughly cut half of the berries in half, and leave the others whole. Combine with the other ingredients in a bowl, gently turning. Set aside for 30 minutes before serving.

Close to serving time, sprinkle the top of the custard with the extra caster sugar. Using a blowtorch, caramelise the sugar. Cool until toffee has set. Serve with the macerated strawberries.

LEMON VERBENA PARFAIT WITH APPLE AND GINGER JUICE AND HONEYCOMB

This dish is inspired by harvesting our own honey from the Four in Hand's roof. The dish is fresh, rich and sweet ... a summer dish at any time of the year.

SERVES 10

INGREDIENTS
fresh honeycomb and sorrel leaves, to serve

LEMON VERBENA PARFAIT
2 litres pouring cream
500ml milk
200g lemon verbena, finely chopped
200g caster sugar
200g liquid glucose
14 egg yolks

APPLE AND GINGER JUICE
3 Granny Smith apples, roughly chopped
3cm knob ginger, peeled and roughly chopped
150ml clear apple juice
lemon juice and salt, to taste

METHOD
To make the lemon verbena parfait, combine the cream, milk and 150g of the lemon verbena in a large saucepan. Bring to a simmer, then turn off the heat and leave for 20 minutes, to infuse.

Reheat gently, and stir in the sugar and glucose until dissolved. Whisk the egg yolks in a bowl. Strain the cream mixture, and while still hot pour onto the egg yolks, whisking constantly. Pour into a clean saucepan and add the remaining lemon verbena. Stir over very low heat until the mixture coats the back of a spoon.

Pour into a bowl sitting on another bowl filled with ice, to stop the cooking. Stir often to release the heat, then place into the fridge until chilled.

Churn in an ice-cream machine according to manufacturer's instructions. Transfer to a 43cm x 30cm x 6cm loaf tin, and freeze until firm.

For the apple and ginger juice, combine the apples, ginger and apple juice in a blender, and blend until smooth. Pass through a fine strainer and add lemon juice and salt to taste. Refrigerate until chilled.

To serve, turn the parfait out of the tin, and cut into slices. Spoon some apple and ginger juice into the serving dishes, add a slice of parfait, and garnish with honeycomb and sorrel leaves.

NOTES
Verbena is a herb that can be grown in the home garden, but it can also be sourced from specialist produce suppliers. Lemon verbena is the type used in cooking and tea, and as the name implies, has a lemony flavour and fragrance.

LEMON THYME RICE PUDDING WITH PASSIONFRUIT CURD AND TOASTED PISTACHIOS

SERVES 8–10

INGREDIENTS
200g pistachio kernels
500ml cream
500ml milk
2 vanilla beans, split
1 bunch lemon thyme
180g arborio rice
200g egg yolks (about 10)
150g caster sugar

PASSIONFRUIT CURD
140g unsalted butter, chopped
30g caster sugar
130ml passionfruit juice (see Note)
4 eggs

METHOD
To make the passionfruit curd, place the butter, sugar and passionfruit juice in a saucepan, and stir over low heat until butter has melted and sugar has dissolved. Lightly beat the eggs in a heatproof metal bowl. Pour the passionfruit mixture over the eggs, and whisk to combine.

Stand the bowl over a pan of simmering water. Whisk every 5 minutes until thickened. Transfer to a cool bowl, and chill before serving.

Preheat the oven to 200°C. Spread the pistachios onto an oven tray, and bake for 4 minutes, until lightly toasted. Cool, then roughly chop.

Combine the cream, milk, vanilla beans and lemon thyme in a saucepan. Bring to the boil. Add the rice and cook for about 30 minutes or until very soft (no bite whatsoever).

Whisk the egg yolks and sugar until light and fluffy. Add to the saucepan, and cook, stirring, over low heat until thick. Cook this as you would a custard — take care not to get the mixture too hot or it will curdle.

Remove the vanilla beans and thyme.

Serve with the passionfruit curd and pistachios.

NOTES
To get the passionfruit juice, scoop the pulp from fresh passionfruit and press through a strainer to remove the seeds. If you want to make the pudding ahead of time, pour into a chilled bowl and refrigerate. Serve cold, or reheat in a non-stick saucepan over a low heat, stirring continuously.

BEETROOT BROWNIE WITH VANILLA AND GINGER CRÈME FRAÎCHE

SERVES 12

INGREDIENTS

450g caster sugar

4 eggs

250g unsalted butter, melted

seeds scraped from 1 vanilla bean

170g plain flour

115g dark cocoa powder

1 tsp salt

150g hazelnuts, roasted and chopped

200g grated beetroot, plus extra to garnish

400g dark chocolate (65%), chopped

200g crème fraîche, to serve

seeds scraped from 1 vanilla bean, extra

5g freshly grated ginger

METHOD

Preheat the oven to 160°C. Lightly grease a 30cm x 25cm x 5cm pan and line with non-stick baking paper.

Use an electric mixer to beat the sugar and eggs to ribbon stage (see Note). Add the butter and vanilla seeds, and beat well. Sift the flour, cocoa powder and salt over the mixture, and fold in until just combined. Fold in the nuts, grated beetroot and chocolate.

Spread into the prepared tray, and bake for 20–30 minutes, until a knife comes out clean when inserted into the centre. Cool, then cut into 12 portions.

Whip the crème fraîche, vanilla seeds and ginger together. To serve the brownies warm, gently reheat in the microwave. Serve with the crème fraîche, garnished with extra beetroot.

NOTE

Ribbon stage is when the mixture is very light, foamy and thick enough to hold its shape for a few seconds when the mixture runs off the beaters onto the mixture in the bowl.

SET CUCUMBER CREAM WITH CUCUMBER GRANITA

A bit left-of-centre for a dessert dish, but a good one nonetheless. It's cooling and refreshing, a cleansing end to a summer lunch.

SERVES 8

INGREDIENTS

1 litre cream
100g caster sugar
2 cucumbers, skin on, chopped
juice of 1 lemon
3½ leaves titanium-strength gelatine
1 cucumber, to garnish

CUCUMBER GRANITA

4 cucumbers, skin on
pinch of salt
200g liquid glucose
200ml fresh Granny Smith apple juice
lemon juice, to taste

METHOD

Stir the cream and sugar in a saucepan over low heat until the sugar has dissolved and the mixture is warm. Add the cucumber and use a stick blender to blend until green. Add the lemon juice.

Soak the gelatine in a bowl of cold water for 5 minutes or until soft. Squeeze out excess water, then add to the warm cream mixture. Stir to dissolve. Strain through a sieve and pour into eight lightly oiled dariole moulds. Place into the fridge to set.

To make the cucumber granita, blend all the ingredients until smooth. Strain and pour into a chilled metal tray. Freeze for 6 hours, or overnight, until solid.

To serve, use a vegetable peeler to shave ribbons from the extra cucumber. Turn the creams out into serving dishes and arrange cucumber ribbons around them. Use a fork to scrape the granita into large crystals, and spoon around the creams.

ROAST PEACHES WITH HOEGAARDEN SNOW

My all-time favourite dessert. Sweet, sour, hot and cold all at the same time, it's one for the big kids.

SERVES 6

INGREDIENTS

HOEGAARDEN SNOW
500ml natural yoghurt
600ml buttermilk
400ml Hoegaarden beer
lemon juice
300g liquid glucose

ROAST PEACHES
6 ripe peaches
100g unsalted butter, melted
150g caster sugar

METHOD

To make the Hoegaarden snow, whisk all the ingredients together and pour into a chilled metal tray.

Freeze overnight, until solid. Remove from the freezer and scrape with a fork into large crystals, then put back into the freezer.

For the roast peaches, preheat the oven to 200°C. Brush the peaches all over with butter, and roll in sugar to coat evenly.

Place into an ovenproof dish and cook for 15 minutes, basting and turning every 5 minutes, until soft.

Spoon the Hoegaarden snow into chilled bowls. Place a peach into each bowl, and drizzle with pan juices.

CRUMBLE WITH POACHED RHUBARB

SERVES 6

INGREDIENTS

CRUMBLE
500g plain flour
250g cold unsalted butter, chopped
250g demerara sugar
100g hazelnuts, crushed
100g rolled oats
pinch of ground cinnamon
pinch of ground ginger
6 tbsp crème fraîche, to serve

POACHED RHUBARB
2 bunches rhubarb, stalks trimmed and diced
600ml ginger beer
20g fresh ginger, peeled and chopped
4 star anise
1 cinnamon stick
1 vanilla bean, split, seeds scraped
200g caster sugar

METHOD

To make the crumble, preheat the oven to 160°C, and grease a 3cm-deep baking tray. Use your fingertips to mix the flour and butter to a sandy texture. Mix in the sugar, then the remaining ingredients.

Spread the crumble into the prepared tray and cook for 10 minutes or until golden. If not using immediately, cool completely, and store in an airtight container.

For the poached rhubarb, place all ingredients into a saucepan (including vanilla bean). Bring to a simmer and cook for 4 minutes, or until the rhubarb is just tender. Transfer to an ovenproof dish and remove the star anise, cinnamon stick and vanilla bean.

Sprinkle the crumble mixture over the rhubarb, and return to the oven for about 5 minutes, to reheat.

Remove from the oven and serve with crème fraîche.

PETITS FOURS – MARSHMALLOW

MAKES ABOUT 100 PIECES

INGREDIENTS
470g caster sugar
1 vanilla bean, split, seeds scraped
3½ leaves titanium-strength gelatine
120g eggwhites (about 3)
150g desiccated coconut

METHOD
Place the sugar into a saucepan and add 300ml water. Stir over low heat until sugar has dissolved, then add the vanilla bean and seeds, increase the heat and bring to the boil. Place a sugar thermometer into the pan and cook until it reaches 128°C.

Meanwhile, soak the gelatine in a bowl of cold water for 5 minutes, or until soft. Squeeze out excess water, then add to the syrup and stir to dissolve. Remove vanilla bean.

Place the eggwhites into the bowl of an electric mixer. Whisk whites until soft peaks form, and with the motor running slowly, pour the hot syrup onto the whites (being careful to avoid the whisk so you don't get splashed with syrup). Increase the speed to medium and keep whisking until the mixture is cold.

Line a 30cm x 25cm x 5cm pan with 2 layers of cling wrap. Pour the marshmallow mixture into the pan, and place into the fridge for about 3 hours, or until set. Lift out of the tray, and use a wet knife to cut into cubes.

Meanwhile, preheat the oven to 160°C. Spread the coconut onto a baking tray and cook for about 5 minutes, stirring occasionally so it cooks evenly, until golden brown. Cool.

Roll the cubes of marshmallow in the coconut to coat. Store in an airtight container for up to 2 weeks.

PETITS FOURS — CHOCOLATE

MAKES ABOUT 100

INGREDIENTS
250g hazelnuts
500g dark chocolate (65%)
250g cream
150g liquid glucose
dark cocoa powder, to dust

METHOD
Preheat the oven to 180°C. Spread the hazelnuts onto an oven tray, and roast for about 7 minutes or until golden (you will be able to see parts where the skin has broken). Tip onto a clean tea towel and rub to remove the skins. Cool, then pick out the nuts.

Break up the chocolate and place into a bowl sitting over a saucepan of just-boiled water (off the heat — and make sure the bottom of the bowl is not touching the water). Once softened, stir until melted and smooth.

In a separate pan, heat the cream and glucose to 60°C (do not let it boil). Pour the cream mixture onto the chocolate, and use a metal spoon to stir until evenly combined and smooth.

Roughly crush the hazelnuts, and stir into the chocolate mixture. Line a 30cm x 25cm x 5cm pan with greaseproof paper, and pour the mixture in. Place into the fridge to cool and set.

Remove from the pan and use a hot knife to cut into small cubes. Place the cocoa powder into a bowl and toss the chocolate cubes through, to coat. Arrange in a shallow airtight container in a single layer and keep in the fridge.

LAVOSH BREAD

SERVES 12

INGREDIENTS

400g plain flour
100g unsalted butter, chopped and softened
15g salt
2 eggs, lightly beaten
100ml milk
assortment of cheeses, to serve

METHOD

Combine the flour, butter and salt in the bowl of an electric mixer and season with freshly ground black pepper. Using a dough hook, mix until combined. Add the eggs and milk, and mix until the mixture just comes together — do not overwork the dough.

Divide the dough into 4 portions, wrap in cling wrap and refrigerate for 2 hours.

Preheat the oven to 160°C. Using a pasta machine, starting at the widest setting, roll a portion of dough once through each setting until you get to number 1 — the dough should be almost see-through. Repeat with remaining portions.

Cut the rolled-out dough into 10cm lengths, and place onto oven trays. Cook in batches for 6–8 minutes, until crisp and golden. Cool completely, then store in an airtight container.

Serve with cheese.

VARIATIONS

For fennel lavosh, dry roast 20g fennel seeds, crush slightly using a mortar and pestle and add to the flour. For thyme lavosh, pick leaves from 1/2 bunch of thyme and add to the flour.

HAY ICE-CREAM

SERVES 8

INGREDIENTS
600ml cream
600ml milk
1 vanilla bean, split, seeds scraped
organic hay (as much as can fit in the pot)
140g caster sugar
12 egg yolks
finely grated zest and juice of 3 lemons

METHOD
Combine the cream, milk, vanilla bean and hay in a saucepan and bring to the boil. Meanwhile, whisk the sugar and eggs yolks together in a bowl until light and creamy.

Strain the cream mixture, and while still hot, pour onto the sugar and egg yolk mixture, whisking constantly. Add the lemon zest and juice.

Pour the mixture into a clean saucepan and stir over low heat until it reaches 82°C–84°C. Remove from the heat and pass through a strainer into a bowl that is sitting on ice, to stop the cooking. Stir often to release the heat. Place into the fridge to chill.

Transfer mixture to an ice-cream machine, and churn according to manufacturer's instructions. Transfer to an airtight container and freeze until serving time.

NOTE
Buy sterilised organic straw from famers' markets or organic grocers to use as hay.

GINGER MERINGUE WITH SORREL SORBET AND POACHED RHUBARB

SERVES 6

INGREDIENTS

1 quantity poached rhubarb (see p. 195) — halve stalks
    instead of dicing

SORREL SORBET

4 Granny Smith apples, cored and roughly chopped
    (skin and all)
500ml clear apple juice
1 bunch sorrel
4 English spinach leaves
200ml liquid glucose

GINGER MERINGUE

180g eggwhites (about 5)
270g caster sugar
seeds scraped from ½ vanilla bean
10g fresh ginger, peeled and finely grated

METHOD

To make the sorrel sorbet, combine the apples, 400ml of the apple juice, the sorrel and spinach leaves in a blender. Blitz until smooth, then strain through a fine strainer. Heat the remaining apple juice and glucose until runny, and whisk into the juice mixture. Place into the fridge to chill.

Pour the mixture into an ice-cream machine and churn according to manufacturer's instructions. Transfer to an airtight container and freeze until serving time.

To make the ginger meringue, put the eggwhites, sugar and vanilla seeds into the bowl of an electric mixer. Sit the bowl over a saucepan of simmering water and, using a wire whisk, stir until the sugar dissolves and the mixture is warm. Place the bowl onto the mixer, and whisk on high speed until the mixture is thick and white. Add the ginger at the last second and whisk until combined.

Fill a 1-litre capacity microwave-safe takeaway container with the meringue, making sure there are no air pockets. Wipe any meringue off the top edge of the container so it will rise evenly. Cook, uncovered, in the microwave for 1 minute on high, then place straight into the fridge. Leave for about 1 hour, to cool.

To serve, place the meringue under a high grill for 1 minute, or until golden. Turn the meringue out onto a wet chopping board, grilled side up, and cut into squares. Arrange poached rhubarb into serving dishes, top with meringue and spoon sorrel sorbet around.

GOAT'S MILK POPSICLES WITH FIGS AND CHERRIES

SERVES 6

INGREDIENTS

GOAT'S MILK POPSICLES
500g goat's milk yoghurt
10g ginger, finely grated
35ml lemon juice
150g liquid glucose

BAKED FRUIT
9 figs, halved
36 cherries
30g caster sugar
1 cinnamon stick
1 star anise
1 vanilla pod, split

METHOD

To make the goat's milk popsicles, whisk the yoghurt, ginger and lemon juice in a bowl. Place into the fridge for 1 hour to infuse.

Warm the glucose in a saucepan until it is a thinner consistency, and stir into the yoghurt mixture. Strain through a fine sieve, then place into the fridge to chill.

Pour the mixture into an ice-cream machine and churn according to manufacturer's instructions.

Transfer to a piping bag, and pipe the ice-cream into six 100–150ml capacity popsicle moulds. When semi-set, stick in wooden sticks until halfway down. Freeze until firm.

To serve, remove from the freezer and allow to melt around the edges very slightly before pulling out of the moulds with a gentle twist.

For the baked fruit, preheat the oven to 200°C. Place the fruit into a small ovenproof dish. Sprinkle the sugar over, and add the cinnamon, star anise and vanilla. Cover with foil, and bake for 8–10 minutes, or until fruit is soft but still holding its shape. Serve drizzled with pan juices, with the popsicles.

PRALINE PEANUT BUTTER BLOCK

SERVES 12

INGREDIENTS
185g caster sugar
15 egg yolks
350g white chocolate
900ml cream
250g smooth peanut butter
50ml cream, extra

PRALINE
125g caster sugar
125g salted roasted peanuts
finely grated zest of ½ orange

METHOD
Place the sugar into a saucepan and add 50ml water. Stir over low heat until sugar has dissolved, then increase the heat and bring to the boil. Place a sugar thermometer into the pan and cook until it reaches 118°C (soft ball stage).

Put the egg yolks into the bowl of an electric mixer and whisk on high until light and fluffy. Reduce the speed to low, and with the motor running, gradually add the sugar syrup. Turn the speed back up to high and whisk until cool.

Break up the chocolate and place into a bowl sitting over a saucepan of simmering water (make sure the bottom of the bowl is not touching the water). Once softened, stir until melted and smooth. Add to the egg mixture and keep whisking until combined.

Whip the cream in a large bowl to form soft peaks. Fold the cream through the egg and chocolate mixture one third at a time. Stir the peanut butter and extra cream together until smooth, and fold into the mixture.

Line a 30cm x 25cm x 5cm pan with a few layers of cling wrap. Pour the mixture into the tray and freeze overnight.

To make the praline, heat the sugar in a saucepan until melted and golden. Stir in the nuts and orange zest. Pour onto an oiled tray and leave to cool and harden. Grind half the praline to a fine texture, and roughly break up the other half by smashing with a rolling pin.

Place a plastic chopping board into the freezer for 30 minutes. Turn the frozen mixture out onto the chilled board, and remove the cling film. Cut into 12 pieces. Roll in the praline to coat, and serve immediately.

APPLE TARTE TATIN WITH CALVADOS CREAM

Everyone should try to make a tarte tartin at least once in their life. The suspense in flipping it over and seeing if it will turn out still gets me to this day.

SERVES 6-8

INGREDIENTS

200g soft butter

200g caster sugar

2 cinnamon sticks, split lengthways

4 star anise

2 vanilla beans, cut into long strips

4 Pink Lady apples, peeled, cored and cut into thick wedges

2 sheets frozen butter puff pastry, thawed

extra caster sugar, to sprinkle

CALVADOS CREAM

100ml cream

100ml crème fraîche

300ml Calvados

½ tsp finely grated lemon zest

squeeze of lemon juice

METHOD

Preheat the oven to 190°C. Line the base of a 20cm (base measurement) ovenproof frying pan with the butter, in an even layer. Sprinkle with the sugar, and scatter the spices over.

Arrange the apple pieces in a single layer over the base, all facing the same way in a clockwise fashion. Lay the pastry sheet over the apples (trimmed and joined to fit neatly), and cut an X in the centre. Sprinkle with the extra sugar.

Place over medium heat until it starts to bubble up the sides of the pan and goes golden brown. Transfer to the oven and cook for 20 minutes. Let sit for 10 minutes before carefully turning out onto a platter or board. Serve with the Calvados cream.

To make the Calvados cream, put the cream and crème fraîche into a bowl, and whisk until soft peaks form. Stir in the Calvados, lemon zest and juice.

APPLE TARTE TATIN WITH CALVADOS CREAM

CHEESECAKE MOUSSE WITH NUT CRUMBLE, MACERATED STRAWBERRIES AND CANDIED GINGER

SERVES 6

INGREDIENTS

CHEESECAKE MOUSSE
220g cream cheese, at room temperature
95g caster sugar
seeds scraped from 1 vanilla bean
240ml cream
95g crème fraîche
35ml lemon juice
Finely grated zest of ½ lemon
Finely shredded mint, to garnish

NUT CRUMBLE
100g plain flour
50g demerara sugar
50g cold unsalted butter, diced
10g slivered almonds
10g pistachios, chopped
10g pumpkin seeds

MACERATED STRAWBERRIES
125g strawberries
2 star anise
15g brown sugar
15ml cabernet sauvignon vinegar (good quality)

CANDIED GINGER
50g fresh ginger, peeled and julienned
200g caster sugar

METHOD

To make the cheesecake mousse, use an electric mixer to whisk the cream cheese, sugar and vanilla seeds together until smooth and thickened. Whip the cream, crème fraîche and lemon juice together until thick. Add the lemon zest. Fold the two mixtures together, and refrigerate for 1 hour, to set.

For the nut crumble, preheat the oven to 170°C. Combine the flour and sugar in a bowl, and add the butter. Use your fingertips to rub the butter into the flour until the mixture is like breadcrumbs. Spread onto a baking tray and bake for 8–10 minutes, or until golden. Cool.

Spread the nuts and seeds onto a baking tray and toast in the oven for about 5 minutes, or until golden. Cool, then mix with the crumble. Store in an airtight container until needed.

For the macerated strawberries, cut the strawberries into quarters. Place into a shallow bowl with the star anise, sprinkle with sugar and drizzle with vinegar. Let sit for 15 minutes before serving.

To make the candied ginger, place the ginger into a small saucepan and cover with cold water. Bring to the boil, then drain. Repeat this step two more times.

Combine the sugar and 200ml water in a small saucepan. Stir over low heat until the sugar has dissolved, then bring to a simmer. Add the ginger, and simmer for 15–20 minutes, until the ginger is transparent. Use a fork to lift out. Drain on a wire rack.

To serve, spoon quenelles of the cheesecake mousse onto plates. Sprinkle nut crumble around, and top with the macerated strawberries and candied ginger. Scatter mint over.

DOUGHNUTS AND CUSTARD

MAKES 30

INGREDIENTS

DOUGHNUTS

275g plain flour

5g salt

35g caster sugar

Finely grated zest of ½ lemon

seeds scraped from ¼ vanilla bean

25g fresh yeast (or 10g dried yeast)

100ml milk

2 eggs

1 egg yolk

35g unsalted butter, just softened

vegetable oil, to deep-fry

100g caster sugar, extra

½ tsp ground cinnamon

CUSTARD

500ml milk

½ vanilla bean, split

70g caster sugar

6 egg yolks

METHOD

For the doughnuts, combine the flour, salt, sugar, lemon and vanilla in the bowl of an electric mixer. Using a dough hook, mix until combined.

Meanwhile, dissolve the yeast in the milk (in a jug), and whisk the eggs and yolks together in a bowl.

With the motor running at low speed, add the yeast mixture to the flour, followed by the egg mixture, then the butter. Mix until a smooth dough forms. Place into a lightly floured bowl, cover with cling wrap and leave in a draught-free place to prove until doubled in size.

Knock back the dough. Weigh out 20g portions of dough and roll into balls. Arrange on a tray, set slightly apart, and cover with lightly oiled cling wrap. Place into the fridge until needed (up to 1 day).

To make the custard, place the milk into a saucepan, add the vanilla bean and bring to the boil. Meanwhile, whisk the sugar and yolks together in a bowl until creamy. Pour ¼ of the milk onto the egg mixture, whisking constantly.

Pour back into the pan with the remaining milk, and stir continuously over low heat until the custard thickens and coats the back of a spoon. Pour into a chilled bowl sitting on a bowl of ice, stirring to release the heat, then refrigerate until cooled.

To finish the doughnuts, remove from the fridge, and stand at room temperature to prove again until doubled in size. Half fill a large saucepan with oil and heat to 170°C. Deep-fry the balls in batches until golden, and drain on paper towels. Combine the extra sugar with the cinnamon, and toss the warm doughnuts in the mixture. Serve with custard.

ETON MESS

SERVES 8

INGREDIENTS

600ml cream, whipped, to serve

MALT ICE-CREAM

250ml milk

1 litre cream

150g liquid glucose

1 vanilla bean, split, seeds scraped

12 egg yolks

100g caster sugar

375g jar liquid malt barley

MERINGUE

270g caster sugar

180g egg whites (about 5)

seeds scraped from ½ vanilla bean

BROWNIE

200g dark chocolate, chopped

125g butter, chopped

2 eggs

225g caster sugar

85g plain flour

60g cocoa powder

1 tsp salt

75g hazelnuts, roasted and chopped

METHOD

To make the malt ice-cream, combine the milk, cream, glucose and vanilla bean and seeds in a saucepan, and bring to the boil. Add the malt. Meanwhile, whisk the yolks and sugar until pale and creamy. Pour about one quarter of the hot milk mixture onto the egg mixture, whisking constantly.

Pour back into the pan with the remaining milk, and stir continuously over low heat until it reaches 82°C on a thermometer. Remove vanilla bean. Pour into a chilled bowl over a bowl of ice to stop the cooking, stirring to release the heat. Place into the fridge to chill.

When the mixture is cold, churn in an ice-cream machine according to manufacturer's instructions. Transfer to an airtight container and freeze until firm.

To make the meringue, preheat the oven to 90°C. Line 2 baking trays with non-stick baking paper. Place the sugar, egg whites and vanilla seeds into the bowl of an electric mixer and place over a saucepan of simmering water, stirring until the sugar has dissolved.

Put the bowl onto the mixer and whisk on high until the mixture is thick and white. Spread the meringue out onto the lined trays until about 1 cm thick. Bake for 4 hours, or until dried and crispy. Cool, then crush and store in an airtight container.

For the brownie, preheat the oven to 160°C, and line a 15cm x 12cm x 5cm pan with baking paper. Melt the chocolate and butter together in a small saucepan or the microwave. Cool. Put the eggs and sugar into the bowl of an electric mixer, and beat to ribbon stage (see Note).

Add the chocolate mixture to the egg mixture and whisk to combine. Fold in the sifted flour, cocoa powder and salt, then the nuts. Spread into the pan, and bake for 20 minutes (it will still be quite soft once cooked). Set aside to cool.

To serve, fold the broken meringue through the whipped cream. Roughly chop the brownie and gently reheat in the microwave until gooey. Layer the meringue and cream mixture, brownie and ice-cream into tall glasses. The aim is to look messy, not neat. Serve immediately.

NOTE

Ribbon stage is when the mixture is very light, foamy and thick enough to hold its shape for a few seconds when the mixture runs off the beaters onto the mixture in the bowl.

BREAKFAST 4 DESSERT

SERVES 6

INGREDIENTS

1 punnet strawberries, hulled and halved
1 punnet raspberries
1 punnet blueberries
½ cup rolled oats, toasted

YOGHURT SORBET

500ml natural yoghurt
1 tbsp liquid glucose
1 vanilla bean, split, seeds scraped
300ml buttermilk
juice of 2 lemons

BERRY GRANITA

2 punnets strawberries, hulled
2 punnets raspberries
1 punnet blueberries
500ml cranberry juice
150g liquid glucose
juice of 2 lemons
¼ bunch mint stalks, bruised
¼ bunch basil stalks, bruised

METHOD

To make the yoghurt sorbet, combine the yoghurt, glucose and vanilla bean and seeds in a saucepan and heat until hot but not boiling. Set aside to cool, and remove vanilla bean. Combine in a bowl with the buttermilk, lemon juice and a pinch of salt. Place into the fridge to chill. Transfer to an ice-cream machine, and churn according to manufacturer's instructions. Transfer to an airtight container and freeze until firm.

To make the berry granita, combine all the ingredients in a saucepan and bring to the boil. Reduce the heat slightly and simmer for 5 minutes. Set aside to cool, remove stalks, then blend until smooth. Pass through a fine strainer. Pour strained liquid into a shallow metal dish, and freeze overnight or until firm.

To serve, arrange berries into chilled bowls and sprinkle with oats. Put a large quenelle of yoghurt sorbet in the middle, and scatter with berry granita.

LIQUORICE QUINCE, JERSEY MILK SORBET AND DOLCE CREAM CHEESE

SERVES 8

INGREDIENTS

SORBET
1 litre Jersey milk
200g caster sugar
1½ tbsp liquid glucose
1 vanilla bean, split, seeds scraped

DOLCE CREAM CHEESE
390g can condensed milk
250g cream cheese
squeeze of lemon juice

LIQUORICE QUINCE
2 quinces
1 litre sugar syrup (see Basics, p. 233)
50g liquorice root

LINSEED CRISPS
100g linseeds
20g potato flour
2g salt

METHOD

To make the sorbet, combine the ingredients in a saucepan and stir over low heat to dissolve the sugar and glucose. Transfer to a bowl and put into the fridge to chill.

Remove the vanilla bean. Pour the mixture into an ice-cream machine and churn according to manufacturer's instructions. Transfer to an airtight container and freeze.

For the dolce cream cheese, place the can of condensed milk on its side into a large saucepan and cover completely with water. Cover the pan with a lid, and bring to the boil. Tilt the lid slightly, and cook for 4 hours, topping up with boiling water as needed (can must be submerged at all times). Cool completely before opening the can.

Measure 100g of the caramelised condensed milk and mix with the cream cheese and lemon juice. Chill until needed.

For the liquorice quince, peel the quinces, keeping the skin. Cut into cubes. Combine in a saucepan with the sugar syrup, along with the skin and the liquorice root. Bring to a gentle simmer, and cook uncovered for about 1 hour, or until tender when tested with the point of a small sharp knife. Use a slotted spoon to lift the quinces from the syrup.

To make the linseed crisps, preheat the oven to 180°C. Place the ingredients into a bowl. Bring 350ml water to the boil and pour into the bowl. Whisk until smooth, and set aside at room temperature to rest for 20 minutes.

Roll between two sheets of baking paper until very thin. Peel off and discard top sheet of paper, and lift mixture on bottom sheet onto a baking tray. Bake for 6–8 minutes, until set. Peel off bottom sheet and return to the oven upside down to finish baking for another 2 minutes. Cool and break into shards.

To serve, reheat the quince cubes in the cooking syrup. Smear some dolce cream cheese onto each plate. Top with a quenelle of sorbet, add a few cubes of quince and shards of linseed crisps.

NOTE
Left-over caramelised condensed milk will keep in a bowl in the fridge for up to 2 weeks.

BASICS

These are the building blocks for any great dish. Once you've mastered the basics, you can add, subtract and explore new ideas to suit your taste.

FLAVOURED SALTS

INGREDIENTS
100g Murray River Salt (pink salt)
Choose one of the following flavourings for the salt:
Sage salt: 15g fresh sage leaves, chopped
Cumin salt: 15g cumin seeds, roasted (see below)
Seaweed salt: 15g dried seaweed, torn
Celery salt: 15g dried celery leaves (see below)
Lemon salt: Finely grated zest of 3 lemons
Fennel salt: 15g roasted fennel seeds (see below)

METHOD
Use a mortar and pestle to grind the salt and flavouring together until well combined. Store in an airtight container.

TO DRY THE CELERY LEAVES
Preheat oven to 60°C. Pick leaves from a bunch of celery, and arrange onto a baking tray. Dry for 1 hour or until crisp. Cool. Weigh and grind with salt as directed.

TO ROAST CUMIN OR FENNEL SEEDS
Place into a dry frying pan, and cook over medium heat for about a minute, or until fragrant. Transfer to a plate to cool. Weigh and grind with salt as directed.

SOY DRESSING

MAKES 1 LITRE

INGREDIENTS
2 star anise
3g coriander seeds
½ cinnamon stick
400ml sugar syrup (see p. 233)
500ml light soy sauce
200ml white wine vinegar
25g ginger, chopped
5 kaffir lime leaves

METHOD
Place the spices into a dry saucepan, and toast over medium heat until fragrant.

Add the remaining ingredients. Bring to a simmer and cook for 5 minutes, then remove from the heat and cool completely. Strain.

NOTE
Place into a clean bottle and store in the fridge for up to 3 months.

SHERRY DRESSING

MAKES 500ML

INGREDIENTS
100ml sherry vinegar
50g sugar
1 sprig thyme
2 black peppercorns
1 bay leaf
400ml olive oil
10ml lemon juice

METHOD
Combine the vinegar, sugar, thyme, peppercorns and bay leaf in a small saucepan and bring to the boil. Set aside to cool.

Whisk in the olive oil and lemon juice, and season with salt and freshly ground black pepper.

NOTE
Place into a clean bottle and store in the fridge for up to 3 months.

VIERGE DRESSING

MAKES 1 LITRE

INGREDIENTS
100g coriander seeds, toasted
2 star anise, toasted
1 litre extra virgin olive oil
3 bunches of basil (leaves and stems)
finely grated zest and juice of 3 lemons

METHOD
Place the coriander seeds, star anise, oil and basil in a blender, and blend until green but not warm.

Add the zest and juice, and season with salt and freshly ground black pepper. Stand for 1 hour to infuse the flavours, then strain through a fine sieve. Transfer to a bottle. Shake well before using.

NOTE
Keep for up to 1 week. To keep longer, omit the lemon juice, and add a little to taste when serving.

PORK SAUCE

MAKES 500ML

INGREDIENTS
2kg pork bones, chopped
splash of olive oil
2 onions, diced
2 carrots, diced
2 celery stalks, diced
400ml cooking port
400ml clear apple juice
1 cinnamon stick
2 star anise
100g fresh ginger, roughly chopped
2 litres chicken stock
1 bunch sage stalks, torn

METHOD
Preheat oven to 200°C. Put the pork bones into a roasting pan and cook for about 30 minutes, until golden brown, but not too dark or they will become bitter.

Heat the oil in a large pot and sweat the vegetables until lightly coloured. Add the port and bring to the boil, then cook until reduced slightly. Add the apple juice and two thirds of the roasted pork bones.

Place the cinnamon and star anise into a dry frying pan and cook over medium heat until fragrant.

Add to the pot, along with three quarters of the ginger and the stock.

Bring to the boil and skim off any impurities. Reduce the heat and simmer uncovered for 4 hours.

Strain through a fine strainer into a clean saucepan. Add the reserved pork bones and ginger, and the sage stalks. Bring to the boil, then reduce to a fast simmer and cook until reduced by half.

Strain through a fine strainer again and place into the fridge. Any fat solids will set on the top. Simply scrape off and discard.

CHICKEN STOCK

MAKES 3 LITRES

INGREDIENTS
5kg chicken wings
2 celery stalks, chopped
1 onion, chopped
2 carrots, chopped
1 bay leaf
1 bunch thyme
6 black peppercorns

METHOD
Place all ingredients into a large pot, and add 10 litres cold water. Bring to the boil, reduce the heat and simmer uncovered for 6 hours, skimming the surface occasionally.

Strain through a sieve to remove the solids. Keep for up to 1 week in the fridge, or divide into useable portions and freeze.

FISH STOCK

MAKES 2.5 LITRES

INGREDIENTS
2kg fish bones
1 onion, chopped
2 celery stalks, chopped
1 garlic bulb, halved
1 fennel bulb, chopped
3g fennel seeds, toasted
1 star anise, toasted
1 bay leaf
½ bunch thyme

METHOD
Place the fish bones into a large pot with the vegetables and herbs, and cover with 3 litres cold water.

Bring to the boil, reduce the heat and simmer uncovered for 20 minutes, skimming the surface occasionally.

Strain through a sieve to remove the solids. Keep for up to 1 week in the fridge, or divide into useable portions and freeze.

VEAL STOCK

MAKES 4 LITRES

INGREDIENTS
5kg chopped veal bones
6 carrots, chopped
6 onions, chopped
1 head of celery, chopped and washed
500ml red wine
500ml port
2 split pig's trotters
3 bay leaves
1 bunch of thyme
3 bulbs of garlic, halved

METHOD
Preheat the oven to 200°C. Place the veal bones into a roasting pan and roast until golden. Add the vegetables, and cook until golden. Make sure the bones don't get too dark or they will be bitter.

Deglaze the pan with wine and port. Transfer to a large pot, and add the trotters, herbs and garlic. Add enough cold water to cover the ingredients by 5cm.

Bring to the boil, reduce the heat and simmer uncovered for 6 hours, skimming the surface occasionally.

Strain through a sieve to remove the solids. Keep for up to 1 week in the fridge, or divide into useable portions and freeze.

LAMB STOCK

MAKES 4 LITRES

INGREDIENTS

3kg lamb bones
500ml white wine
2 onions, diced
2 carrots, diced
2 garlic cloves, diced
3 celery stalks, chopped
2 bay leaves
1 bunch thyme
1 handful of hay (see Note)

METHOD

Preheat the oven to 200°C. Place two thirds of the lamb bones into a roasting pan and roast until golden. Transfer to a large pot, and deglaze the pan with the white wine. Add to the pot with the vegetables, bay leaves and thyme.

Add enough cold water to cover the ingredients by 5cm and bring to the boil. Reduce the heat and simmer for 3 hours, skimming the surface occasionally.

Add the remaining bones and hay. Simmer for 10 minutes. Strain through a sieve to remove the solids. Refrigerate until needed.

Keep for up to 1 week in the fridge, or divide into useable portions and freeze.

NOTE
Buy sterilised organic straw from farmers' markets or organic grocers.

HAM HOCK STOCK

MAKES 4 LITRES

INGREDIENTS

3 medium ham hocks
1½ carrots, roughly chopped
1½ onions, roughly chopped
2 stalks celery, roughly chopped
1 bay leaf
a few thyme sprigs
¾ tsp black peppercorns

METHOD

Place the hocks into a large stockpot. Add the vegetables, herbs and peppercorns, and enough water so the hocks are completely submerged. Bring to the boil, then reduce the heat so the water is simmering.

Cook uncovered for about 2½ hours, or until the meat is falling off the bone. Let the hocks cool in the stock. Lift the hocks from the stock, pull the meat from the bones and use as required in recipes.

Strain stock through a sieve to remove the solids. Keep for up to 1 week in the fridge, or divide into useable portions and freeze.

BASIC MAYONNAISE

MAKES ABOUT 4 CUPS

INGREDIENTS
6 egg yolks
1 tbsp Dijon mustard
50ml white wine vinegar
500ml vegetable oil
500ml olive oil

METHOD
Put the yolks, mustard and vinegar into the bowl of an electric mixer and whisk until combined.

With the motor running, slowly add the oils in a thin stream. Season with salt and white pepper to taste.

Keep in the fridge for up to a week.

SUGAR SYRUP

MAKES 4 CUPS

INGREDIENTS
500ml water
500g caster sugar

METHOD
Combine the sugar and water in a saucepan, and stir over low heat until sugar has dissolved. Bring to the boil and then remove from heat immediately. Let cool and use as needed.

NOTE
You can infuse the syrup with a split vanilla bean, a cinnamon stick and/or a whole star anise if desired. Keep in the fridge for up to 3 months.

ACKNOWLEDGEMENTS

THIS BOOK HAS BEEN SOME TIME IN THE MAKING AND SO THERE ARE A NUMBER OF PEOPLE I WISH TO THANK:

Photographer Alan Benson and stylist Jane Hann, designer Sarah Odgers, Melissa Leong and recipe editor Tracy Rutherford, thank you for your hard work — you all went above and beyond. To Nikki Christer, my publisher at Random House Australia, and Kate Witenden, project manager — thank you for developing my ideas from scrawled notes on a big black notepad to a printed book. To my agent, Sara Eastwood, thank you for your ongoing support and commitment.

I would like to thank the apprentices, chefs de partie, sous, and Head chefs, past and present from both the Four in Hand and 4Fourteen. Also all the bar staff and kitchen hands — especially JD — I love you. Thank you to the floor staff; in particular, Ollie, Stephen, Raurri, Camilla and Jordan.

The locals of the Four in Hand and loyal supporters and pork eaters of the restaurant, you know who you are. You have all participated in some way to the realisation of *Four Kitchens* — thank you for supporting my dream and inspiring me each night in the kitchen.

Hats off to our fantastic suppliers: Vic's Meats, JOTO, Flinders Island Meat, Say Cheese, Spring Bay Mussels, Regal Salmon, Martin Boetz, Single Origin Coffee, Mitch and Kylie from PorkStar, Moffat, Steve for his oysters, Tim for his venison, Iggy for the bread, our plate designer Glen Tebble, Nicholson and Saville, and Jenny from the Alaskan Crab Co.

Thank you to my friends, who are scattered all over the world but continue to stand by me. In particular, thank you to my teacher Matt Fleming, Big Joe Pav, the Channel 7 crew (front and back), Sharon and Evie and Andrew McConnell and his team. To Liam Tomlin, Raymond Blanc, Gordon Ramsay and Stuart Gillies for all kicking my ass, and the Three Amigos — Warren, Justin, Matt.

To my wonderful family, thank you. To my mum and dad, who inspired me to start cooking and continue to inspire today. Andrew and Cluny, Eliane and Grace, Carol and Kevin, Tommy Egan, thank you for your continued support. Thank you to Joe Saleh and Paul Bard for allowing me to be part of the Four in Hand family and to Andrew Perry, thank you for the cheese room. Very importantly, a massive thank you to Carla Jones, as without her help this book would not have been possible.

Finally to my long-suffering family; being married to me is not easy or glamorous! Thank you to my wife Jane and my beautiful daughters, Lily and Maeve. Your love and support make me do what I do every day.

INDEX

An Ebury Press book
Published by Penguin Random House Australia
Pty Ltd
Level 3, 100 Pacific Highway, North Sydney
NSW 2060
www.penguin.com.au

First published by Ebury Press in 2014

Addresses for companies within the
Random House Group can be found at
www.randomhouse.com.au/offices

National Library of Australia
Cataloguing-in-Publication entry
Fassnidge, Colin, author.
Four Kitchens : beautiful, mouth-watering,
restaurant-quality food to cook at home / Colin
Fassnidge.
ISBN 978 0 85798 234 6 (Hbk.)
Cooking, Australian.
641.5994

Cover and internal design by Sarah Odgers
Cover and internal photography by Alan Benson
Image of brick wall courtesy Shutterstock.com
Styling by Jane Hann
Project food editing by Tracy Rutherford
Recipe preparation by Colin Fassnidge and
Carla Jones
Index by Puddingburn Publishing Services
Printed and bound in China by RR Donnelley